MASSACHUSETTS ARMS COMPANY PERCUSSION REVOLVER
Made at Chicopee Falls, Massachusetts, 1858, with Maynard primer.

AMERICAN FIREARMS
MAKERS

AMERICAN FIREARMS
MAKERS

When, Where, and What They Made

From the Colonial Period to the End of
the Nineteenth Century

A. MERWYN CAREY

THOMAS Y. CROWELL COMPANY : NEW YORK

MANUFACTURED IN THE UNITED STATES OF AMERICA
BY THE VAIL-BALLOU PRESS, INC., BINGHAMTON, NEW YORK

To Edna

Whose help, research, and encouragement over the years made this book possible—as in everything else.

INTRODUCTION

WHEN THE AUTHOR suggested that I write an introduction to this work, it was, to me, a high compliment. I have known the author for more years than he or I care to admit publicly, lest we be dated. And, having read and re-read the manuscript, I was more in a mood to write an appreciation of the effort than an introduction. This because, to me, it is a book to which a foreword is superfluous, yet for which an appreciation should be written by one far better and more worthy than I. What can be said in advance about a biographical cyclopedia of American firearms makers which is, beyond any shadow of doubt, the most definitive ever attempted and ever published? The documentation is correct; the entire work, from first to last, is a labor of love which, I happen to know, has extended over a period of more than thirty years.

Merwyn Carey knows, I think, more antiquarians and dealers both here and abroad than any man of my acquaintance. He has known them intimately, socially and in business. Guns and gunsmiths have been his avocation since his enlistment in the regular army and as a commissioned officer in the first A.E.F. of 1917.

So much for the background of the man who has written, compiled, researched, and created this book. Now let us consider the guns made by the gunsmiths listed in it. If an item of furniture sells anywhere at auction for three thousand dollars, that is big news. If a piece of silver by Paul Revere sells for three thousand dollars, it is often front-page news. Does anything comparable happen in gun collecting? Yes, but without fanfare. It seems gun collectors shun publicity. Theirs is a sort of "top drawer" collecting that just is not talked about to people not in the fraternity. Most antique collectors will start talking about their pursuit at the drop of a word. Gun collectors are clams, unless the other party happens to know at least the nomenclature of guns and gun collecting. Then, and then only, will you learn that a Patterson Colt revolving pistol will bring over three thousand dollars almost anywhere, any time, by just passing along the word that one is available. If you know anything about antique glass, you know that what is called "Stiegel" brings fabulous prices. Now which would you take if you had your choice, a blue Stiegel sugar bowl with cover, or a pre-Revolutionary American rifled barrel gun marked "W. HENRY, LANCASTER"? You want the Stiegel sugar bowl? Thank you! I'll take the rifle!

Mr. Carey has created a readable contribution to the biography of our most important artificers, our gunsmiths. Here you will find them named, dated, and placed from the days when Eltweed Pomeroy was gunsmith (armorer) to the Pilgrim Company, right down to the War Between the States. Mr. Carey does justice to all. Yet when I first read his manuscript it was with the same skepticism with which I had approached all other alleged definitive and documented data lists of American gunsmiths. As it happens, I come from a family who were among the early makers of Pennsylvania rifles in the Conestoga Valley of Pennsylvania where the American rifle was born. I have enough of the family history to serve as a standard by which I can judge the research of others. Mr. Carey has it right. Just as my old tutor used to say of the judging of a dictionary, "If it has yclept, ytouked, ytented and relict in it, the chances are it is a good dictionary." So I have judged this work for correctness in terms of how he handled the considerable number of gunsmiths named Drepperd who happen to have worked jointly and severally at Lancaster, Pennsylvania, from 1777 to 1870.

How Mr. Carey assembled his data makes interesting reading. Since he may not reveal this phase of his work, let me say that he has researched directories of record, published in cities and towns where gunsmiths are known to have worked. How he separated the men employed in the Springfield Arsenal (all of whom are listed as gunsmiths in one directory) from the actual master gunsmiths I do not know, but of this I am sure; he did not do it by gazing into a crystal, as so many gun book authors seem to have done. And finally he has examined, studied, and appraised thousands of American firearms—rifles, muskets, pistols. Here he has presented his fact finding in a form that enables one to refer quickly to specific names, or to study at one's leisure the entire gamut of gunsmiths. Here, then, are the artisans, mechanics, and scientific producers who made the tools of freedom and the guideposts of the frontier. Only a fool would call these men—these gunsmiths—warmongers. They made the guns that won wars, true; but, more than that, they made the guns that protected the pioneer and kept him alive. The arms these men made were *peacemakers*. Even our latest and most terrible arm, the atomic bomb, in *our* hands is a weapon of peace and a peacemaker.

My heartiest congratulations to Mr. Carey, and, on behalf of all antiquarians and all Americana collectors, my heartfelt thanks to him for having completed this work.

CARL W. DREPPERD

FOREWORD

No BOOK ON American Firearms Makers will ever be complete. New evidence and data is continually coming from old firearms and records that are being found from time to time.

This book represents 32 years of careful and diligent research, collecting and inspecting old firearms. Its purpose is to help complete the record.

It is your book, your property, your basic record, and the format is such that your findings can be added under the proper classification. If you should find a piece with a name that is not listed, and the markings of the maker are clear, and you have researched his place of fabrication and the years he made arms, then enter your findings under the proper listing.

Thus, ultimately, a more complete record is possible of American Firearms Makers.

A. MERWYN CAREY

GRATEFUL ACKNOWLEDGMENT

to

Herbert A. Sherlock for his drawings

Mary Jane Gilmore for typing, editing and compiling the manuscript

William Rhoades for typography advice

LIST OF ILLUSTRATIONS

Following page 146

North Flintlock Pistol, U.S. Model of 1813
Aston Percussion Pistol, U.S. Model of 1842
Colt Dragoon, Second U.S. Model of 1848
Deringer Percussion Pistol
Springfield Percussion Pistol (or Carbine)
Springfield Armory, 1860
Volcanic Repeating Fire-Arms Advertisement

Abbey & Co., F. J. 1871–1875. Plant located at 45 South Clark Street, Chicago, Illinois, made percussion and breech-loading arms.

Abbey, George T. 1858–1874. Shop located at Chicago, Illinois, made heavy percussion rifles.

Adams Revolving Arms Co. 1861–1865. Made the English patent of the Adams Percussion Revolver, dated November 7, 1857. Made at the Massachusetts Arms Co. plant at Chicopee Falls, Massachusetts. The Adams Revolving Arms Co. office was in New York, New York. Made Army and Navy models, double-action percussion revolvers bought under contract by the Federal Government during the Civil War. The English-made models, same patent, were sold to the Confederate States.

Adirondack Firearms Co. 1872–1875. Plant located at Plattsburgh, New York, made lever-action, repeating metallic cartridge rifles under the O. M. Robinson Patent. Sold to **Winchester Repeating Arms Co.** in 1875.

Aetna Arms Co. 1880–1890. Plant located in New York City, New York, made 7-shot tip-up brass frame metallic cartridge revolvers.

Afflerbach, William 1860–1866. Shop located at Philadelphia, Pennsylvania, made derringer type of percussion pistol.

Ager, Alexander 1848–1886. Percussion rifle maker at Rumley, Ohio.

Agnew, Andrew 1872–1875. Shop located at Orange, New Jersey, made percussion rifles and did general gunsmithing.

Albertson, Douglas & Co. 1840–1860. Plant located at New London, Connecticut, made whaling percussion guns principally.

Albrecht, Andrew 1779–1782. Gunsmith at Warwick Township, Lancaster County, Pennsylvania, made flintlock Kentucky rifles.

Albright, Henry 1740–1792. Shop located at Lancaster, Pennsylvania. General gunsmith, made flintlock Kentucky rifles.

Alden, E. B. 1863–1868. Shop at Claremont, New Hampshire, made percussion rifles and shotguns.

Aldenderfer, M. 1763–1817. Gunsmith at Lancaster, Pennsylvania, made flintlock Kentucky rifles.

Allbright, T. J. 1845–1870. Shop located at 74 Chestnut Street, St. Louis, Missouri, maker of heavy percussion plains rifles.

Allen, Brown & Luther 1848–1858. Frederick Allen, Andrew J. Brown, and John Luther, plant located at Worcester, Massachusetts, made barrels, mostly smoothbore.

Allen, C. B. 1836–1855. Plant located at Springfield, Massachusetts, made the Elgin Pistol Cutlass for the United States Navy, a short, heavy cutlass with percussion pistol mounted on top of blade. Allen also made the Cochran turret percussion revolvers and rifles.

Allen, Ethan 1834–1871. Ethan Allen was born at Bellingham, Massachusetts, in 1810 and secured his first United States patent for the pepperbox type of multiple firing pistol in 1834. With his brother-in-law, Charles T. Thurber, he established **Allen & Thurber** located at Grafton, Massachusetts, 1837 to 1842, moved to Norwich, Connecticut, 1842 to 1847, and then moved to Worcester, Massachusetts, 1847 to 1856. In 1856 he dissolved the partnership and formed another partnership with another brother-in-law, Thomas

1

P. Wheelock, under the name of **Allen & Wheelock**. They made improved patent pepperboxes at Worcester, Massachusetts, 1856 to 1865. On January 18, 1857, Ethan Allen received a United States patent for a .44 caliber percussion revolver and secured a United States Government contract for 500 Army models in 1861. In 1865 the name was changed to **Ethan Allen & Co.**, making pepperboxes, underhammer pistols, revolvers and rifles. Ethan Allen died in 1871, and his sons-in-law carried on the business under the name of **Forehand & Wadsworth**.

Allen, G. F. 1852–1855. Shop located at Utica, New York, made percussion hunting rifles.

Allen, Henry 1812–1820. Located at 34 Maiden Lane, New York, New York.

Allen, Oliver about 1860. Shop at Norwich, Connecticut.

Allen, Silas 1796–1843. Born 1775 in Boston, Massachusetts, opened a gunshop at Shrewsbury, Massachusetts, in 1796, made flintlock muskets and flintlock Kentucky-type rifles and did general gunsmithing. Closed shop in 1843 and died in 1850.

Allen, Thomas 1768–1785. Shop in New York.

Allen, W. C. 1853–1871. General gunsmith and dealer at 136 Montgomery Street, San Francisco, California. In 1856, moved to 146 Clay Street.

Allen, William 1801–1812. Shop at 108 Maiden Lane, New York, New York, made flintlock fowling pieces and rifles and did general gunsmithing.

Allin, E. S. 1829–1878. Born at Enfield, Connecticut, in 1809, entered Springfield Arsenal, Springfield, Massachusetts, as an apprentice in 1829, became master armorer in 1864. Developed the Allin alteration method of converting flintlock to percussion and also patented a breech-loading carbine. Retired in 1878.

Allison, Thomas about 1810. General gunsmith at Pittsburgh, Pennsylvania.

Alsop, C. R. 1858–1866. Under government contract made Army and Navy model percussion revolvers, patented July 17, 1860. Plant located at Middletown, Connecticut.

Amadon, L. 1861–1867. Shop located at Bellows Falls, Vermont, made percussion hunting rifles and shotguns.

American Arms Co. 1861–1904. Plant located at Chicopee Falls, Massachusetts, 1861 to 1897. Office at 103 Milk Street, Boston, Massachusetts, 1866 to 1893. Under government contract made Smith Patent percussion breech-loading carbines, Henry F. Wheeler Patent (October 31, 1865) multi-barrel metallic cartridge pistols and Whitmore Patent shotguns. Moved plant to Milwaukee, Wisconsin, 1897 to 1904.

American Standard Tool Co. 1860–1881. Plant at Newark, New Jersey, made percussion pistols and tip-up metallic cartridge revolvers.

Ames, George about 1835. Maker of percussion rifles and fowling pieces at Portland, Maine.

Ames, John 1776–1803. Born 1738. A major in the Revolutionary War. Established a gunsmithery at West Bridgewater, Massachusetts, in 1776 fabricating flintlock muskets. He had two sons, David and Oliver. David Ames, born 1761, worked in his father's gunshop and became an expert gunsmith. Commissioned by President Washington, became the first Superintendent of Springfield Arsenal, Springfield, Massachusetts, from 1795 to 1802, when he returned to his father's shop. John Ames died in 1803. The two brothers, David and Oliver, carried on the business at Bridgewater, Massachusetts, until 1806, when they moved to North Easton, Massachusetts. The shop was closed when David Ames died in 1847.

Ames Manufacturing Co. 1834–1847. Nathan Peabody Ames and his brother, James Tyler Ames, founded the company at Chicopee Falls, Massachusetts, in 1834. They manufactured swords, sabers, cutlasses, and bayonets, and cast cannon. Their first government firearms contract was for the Jenks Carbines and Rifles Patent of 1838. In 1843 they received a contract from the Navy for a box-lock percussion pistol known as Navy Model 1843. Nathan Peabody Ames died April 23, 1847. James Tyler Ames succeeded him as head of the firm. From 1834 to 1910 their successive company names were **Ames Mfg. Co., Ames Arms Co., N. P. Ames Co.,** and **The Ames Sword Co.**

Amoskeag Mfg. Co. 1860–1864. Plant located at Manchester, New Hampshire, had a number of government percussion rifle contracts during the Civil War.

Amsby & Harrington about 1864. Located at Worcester, Massachusetts.

Amsden, B. W. 1850–1870. Gunsmith at Saratoga Springs, New York, made custom-built target and match percussion rifles. His son, John Amsden, carried on from 1870 to 1873.

Anderson, James 1775–1778. Recorded as a militia gunsmith in Wil-liamsburg, Virginia. Was armorer for Virginia Colony.

Andrews, Eben about 1840. General gunsmith, shop at Fanueil Hall, Boston, Massachusetts.

Andrews, Edward W. 1825–1860. Made percussion rifles and shotguns. Shop located at 26 Bank Street, Cleveland, Ohio, from 1825 to 1855 and at Oberlin, Ohio, 1855 to 1860.

Andrews, Philip B. 1820–1833. Shop at Cleveland, Ohio, 1820 to 1833, moved to Detroit, Michigan, in 1833.

Andrews & Osborne 1847–1851. Plant located at Canton, Connecticut, from 1847 to 1850, then to Southbridge, Massachusetts, 1850 and 1851, made percussion underhammer pistols and pepperboxes.

Angel, Joseph 1840–1848. General gunsmith at 30 State Street, New Haven, Connecticut.

Angstadt, Peter 1770–1777. Maker of Kentucky flintlock rifles and pistols, shop at Lancaster, Pennsylvania.

Angush, James about 1775. Kentucky flintlock rifle maker at Lancaster, Pennsylvania.

Annely, Edward and Thomas 1748–1777. Gunsmiths and armorers in the New Jersey Militia Revolutionary War service.

Anschutz, E. about 1860. Shop in Philadelphia, Pennsylvania, made heavy match and target percussion rifles.

Anson, Comstock 1869–1875. Percussion rifle maker at Danbury, Connecticut.

Anstadt, Jacob about 1815. Kentucky flintlock rifle maker, shop located at Kutztown, Pennsylvania.

Ansted, A. & J. about 1810. Made flintlock pistols for the Pennsylvania Militia, location of shop not known.

Antis, William 1775–1782. Shop at Fredericktown, Pennsylvania, 1775 to 1781, moved to Mahoning, Pennsylvania, 1781 and 1782. Made Kentucky flintlock rifles and flintlock muskets.

Areis, Francis about 1830. General gunsmith at 60 South Street, Philadelphia, Pennsylvania.

Armstrong, Allen about 1800. Kentucky flintlock rifle and pistol maker at Philadelphia, Pennsylvania.

Armstrong, John, Sr., and John, Jr. 1790–1855. John, Sr., established a gunsmithery at Emmetsburg, Maryland, 1790 to 1827. At the time of John, Sr.'s death in 1827, John, Jr., moved shop to Gettysburg, Pennsylvania, 1827 to 1855. Made flintlock and later percussion rifles.

Armstrong, S. F. about 1880. Made metallic cartridge revolvers at Adamsville, Michigan.

Ashfield, J. about 1835. Shop at Carroll Street, Buffalo, New York. Made percussion hunting rifles.

Ashmore, R., & Son about 1800. Kentucky flintlock rifle makers, shop located Lancaster County, Pennsylvania.

Astol, J. & W. 1805–1812. Makers and importers of pairs of flintlock dueling pistols in cases. Shop at New Orleans, Louisiana.

Aston, Henry 1844–1852. Born in London, England, in 1803. Emigrated to United States in 1819 and worked for Simeon North at Middletown, Connecticut. Started in business for himself at Middletown, Connecticut, in 1844 and received his first government contract February 25, 1845, making Model 1842 Army percussion pistols. Name changed to H. Aston & Co. 1850, closed in 1852.

Aston, William A. 1850–1854. Shop located at Middletown, Connecticut, made underhammer percussion pistols.

Atmar, Ralph about 1800. General gunsmith at 95 Broad Street, Charleston, South Carolina.

Augustine, Samuel 1853–1856. Gunsmith at Athens, Ohio, made percussion rifles.

Austin, Cornelius 1776–1778. Armorer for New Jersey Militia during Revolutionary War service.

Austin, Thomas 1774–1778. Shop at Charlestown, Massachusetts, made flintlock muskets.

Avery, G. about 1780. Kentucky flintlock rifle maker at Hamburg, Pennsylvania.

Axer, John about 1845. Maker of Kentucky percussion rifles in Lancaster County, Pennsylvania.

NOTES

Babbitt, L. W. 1832–1838. Shop located at 14 Bank Street, Cleveland, Ohio, maker of percussion rifles.

Babcock, Moses 1777–1781. Gunsmith at Charlestown, Massachusetts, maker of flintlock muskets.

Backhouse, Richard 1774–1781. Made Kentucky flintlock rifles, shop at Easton, Pennsylvania.

Bachner Brothers 1869–1880. Gun shop at Minneapolis, Minnesota, makers of percussion and metallic cartridge hunting and match rifles.

Bacon, Thomas K. 1852–1891. Shop located at Norwich, Connecticut, 1852 and 1853. Name changed to **Bacon Arms Co.** 1853 to 1855 and **Bacon Manufacturing Co.** 1855 to 1891. Made percussion pistols and pepperboxes, and had United States Government contract for Army and Navy metallic cartridge revolvers under the C. W. Hopkins patent (May 27, 1862).

Bacon, William about 1840. General gunsmith and dealer at 213 Water Street, New York, New York.

Badger, George A. 1865–1868. Maker of percussion rifles and shotguns at Concord, New Hampshire.

Bailey, G. L. 1850–1860. Shop at Portland, Maine, made percussion hunting rifles, also smoothbore long guns.

Bailey, Lebbeus about 1840. General gunsmith at Portland, Maine.

Bailey, Nathan 1776–1779. Made flintlock muskets at New London, Connecticut, for Connecticut militia.

Bailey, Robert about 1777. General gunsmith at York, Pennsylvania.

Bailey, Thomas 1858–1865. Located at New Orleans, Louisiana, made percussion rifles and revolvers.

Baird, S. S. about 1850. Gunsmith at Chittenden, Vermont, made percussion hunting rifles.

Baker, Jacob 1820–1833. General gunsmith and flintlock Kentucky rifle maker at 516 North Front Street, Philadelphia, Pennsylvania.

Baker, John 1837–1850. Shop at Newburgh, New York, made flintlock and, later, percussion rifles.

Baker, John about 1830. Maker of flintlock muskets, gunshop at Germantown, Pennsylvania.

Baker, John 1768–1775. Made Kentucky flintlock rifles, shop at Providence, Pennsylvania.

Baker, Joshua about 1750. Gunsmith at Lancaster, Pennsylvania.

Baker, Melchoir 1779–1805. Gunsmith located in Fayette County, Pennsylvania, made Kentucky flintlock rifles.

Baker & Co., W. H. 1865–1880. Plant at Marathon near Batavia, New York, made heavy percussion target and match rifles, also metallic cartridge rifles.

Baldwin, Aaron about 1840. General gunsmith at 58 Bank Street, Newark, New Jersey.

Baldwin, Elihu 1775–1777. Made flintlock muskets for the Connecticut Colony Militia, shop at Branford, Connecticut.

Ball, Albert 1863–1867. Patented the Ball Magazine Carbine, June 23, 1863, at Worcester, Massachusetts, and moved to Windsor, Vermont, where the carbines were made under United States Government contract at the plant of E. G. Lamson & Co.

Ballantine, John and Patrick 1720–1735. Gunsmiths at Charleston, South Carolina.

Ball & Williams 1861–1868. Made the Ballard Patent, November 5, 1861, breech-loading carbine under United States Government contract, plant at Worcester, Massachusetts.

Ballard Arms Co. 1863–1868. Plant at Fall River, Massachusetts, made the Ballard patent, November 5, 1861, breech-loading carbine under United States Government contracts.

Ballard & Co., C. H. 1861–1872. Made the Ballard Patent, November 5, 1861, breech-loading carbine under United States Government contract, plant at Worcester, Massachusetts, 1860 to 1870. Company name changed to **Ballard & Fairbanks,** 1870 to 1872, plant (same location) made derringer-type metallic cartridge pistols.

Ballweg, A. 1868–1872. Shop at Indianapolis, Indiana. Maker of percussion rifles.

Balsley, Christian about 1795. Flintlock Kentucky rifle maker, Dickinson Township, Cumberland County, Pennsylvania.

Bannon, William about 1875. General gunsmith at Fredericksburg, Virginia.

Barent, Covert 1646–1650. Gunsmith at New Amsterdam (New York, New York).

Barger, Fredric N. 1836–1881. Maker of percussion rifles and smooth-bores, shop at Concord, Ohio.

Barker, F. A. 1861–1865. Had Confederate States Government Contract for percussion muskets and side arms. Plant at Fayetteville, North Carolina.

Barnes, Thomas 1791–1800. Gunsmith at North Brookfield, Massachusetts, made flintlock muskets.

Barnhart, George 1818–1844. Born in Pennsylvania in 1798, son of a Hessian soldier of the Revolutionary War who settled here after the war. In 1818, set up a gunsmithery at Jackson, Ohio. Made fine Kentucky flintlock rifles. Died February 17, 1844.

Barnhart, Nehmiah 1851–1888. Nephew of George Barnhart, shop located at Hallsville, Ohio. Made percussion rifles and shotguns.

Barns, Luther 1800–1810. General gunsmith at 441 North Third Street, Philadelphia, 1800 to 1807 then moved to 8 Fayette Street, Philadelphia, Pennsylvania.

Barr, William about 1845. General gunsmith 106 Beekman Street, New York, New York.

Barrett, J. B. 1857–1863. Gunsmith at Wytheville, Virginia, general gunsmith and percussion hunting rifles and shotguns.

Barrett, Lockhart 1858–1868. Shop at Brattleboro, Vermont, made percussion rifles.

Barrett, Samuel 1775–1800. Maker of flintlock muskets, shop at Concord, Massachusetts.

Barstow, I. & C. (Brothers) 1808–1812. Had United States Government contract for Model 1808 Army flintlock muskets. General gunsmiths, shop located at Exeter, New Hampshire.

Bartlett, A. 1760–1808. Shop near Boston, Massachusetts, made flintlock muskets.

Bartlett, I. about 1815. General gunsmith, Devonshire Street, Boston, Massachusetts.

Bartlett, Joseph & Robert (Brothers) 1825–1847. Made percussion hunting rifles and shotguns. Shop at Chenango (near Binghamton), New York.

Basler, A. L. 1857–1859. Shop at Cincinnati, Ohio, general gunsmith and percussion rifles.

Basinait, Louis about 1860. General gunsmith on Main Street, Albion, New York.

Batcheller, James about 1855. General gunsmith at Madison, Wisconsin.

Batchelor, William about 1805. Shop at 85 Water Street, Philadelphia, Pennsylvania. General gunsmith.

Bateman, Thomas about 1845. General gunsmith at Twelfth Street, St. Louis, Missouri.

Bauer, George 1770–1783. Kentucky flintlock rifle maker at Lancaster, Pennsylvania.

Baum, Samuel about 1820. Flintlock Kentucky rifle maker in Mahoning Township, Columbia County, Pennsylvania.

Baumann, Jacob about 1840. General gunsmith at 73 Second Street, St. Louis, Missouri.

Beach, C. H. 1835–1850. Shop at Celina, Ohio, made Kentucky percussion rifles.

Beals, Fordyce 1858–1863. Patented percussion revolver, September 26, 1854, made at Ilion, New York.

Bean, Russell about 1770. Gunsmith near Jonesboro, Tennessee, made flintlock Kentucky rifles.

Beardsley Mfg. Co. about 1866. Plant at Brooklyn, New York, made percussion rifles.

Beauchee, Francis about 1810. General gunsmith and dealer at Charleston, South Carolina.

Bechtler, Christopher 1829–1874. Born in Germany. Emigrated to the United States in 1829, settled at Rutherford, North Carolina, and established a general gunsmithery. Among other arms he made was a two-barrel percussion pistol with two hammers and two triggers set at an angle so that one barrel was used as a butt as the other barrel was discharged.

Beck, Christian about 1840. General gunsmith on Fifth Street, Cincinnati, Ohio.

Beck, Gideon 1780–1788. Kentucky flintlock rifle maker at Lancaster, Pennsylvania.

Beck, Isaac 1829–1835. Shop at Mifflinberg, Pennsylvania, made Kentucky flintlock rifles.

Beck, John 1772–1777. Maker of Kentucky flintlock rifles at Lancaster, Pennsylvania.

Beck, John Philip 1785–1811. Located in Dauphin County, Pennsylvania, made Kentucky flintlock rifles. In Independence Hall in Philadelphia there is a J. P. Beck flintlock Pennsylvania rifle inscribed, "To the President George Washington AD 1791."

Beck, Valentine 1764–1791. Established a gunsmithery at Bethabara, North Carolina Colony.

Beckley, Elias, Sr. & Jr. 1807–1828. Elias, Sr., had a general gunshop at Berlin, Connecticut, 1807 to 1815. On his death, Elias, Jr., caried on at the same location, 1815–1828.

Becker, J. about 1810. Shop at Lebanon, Pennsylvania, made Kentucky flintlock rifles.

Beebe 1846–1850. Made percussion sawhandle pistols at Albany, New York.

Beebe, Richard 1853–1870. General gunsmith at Springfield, Ohio, made percussion hunting rifles and shotguns.

Beerstecher, Frederick 1840–1860. Maker of Kentucky percussion rifles, shop at Lewisburg, Pennsylvania. Also, patented (September 25, 1855) two-shot derringer-type pistol, one load behind the other with an adjustable hammer to fire the two separate cap cones.

Beig, S. about 1790. Gunsmith in Lancaster County, Pennsylvania, made Kentucky flintlock rifles.

Bekeart, Francis about 1845. General gunsmith at 118 Fulton Street, New York, New York.

Belknap, Leverett about 1850. General gunsmith at 145 Front Street, Hartford, Connecticut.

Bell, John 1745–1754. Gunsmith at Boston, Massachusetts Bay Colony, made flintlock muskets.

Bell, John about 1800. Flintlock Kentucky rifle maker at Carlisle, Pennsylvania

Beman about 1775. Armorer for Massachusetts Militia, location of shop not recorded.

Bemis, Edmund 1746–1785. Shop at Boston, Massachusetts, maker of flintlock muskets and fowling pieces.

Bender, John about 1815. General gunsmith at Lancaster, Pennsylvania.

Benfer, Amos about 1830. Shop located at Beaverstown, Pennsylvania, made Kentucky flintlock rifles.

Bennett, about 1635. One of the early gunsmiths and armorers in the Maryland Colony. Gunsmithery on Kent Island.

Bennett, Daniel K. 1856–1868. Made percussion rifles and shotguns at Montpelier, Vermont.

Bennett, E. A. about 1835. General gunsmith at Waterville, Maine.

Bennett, John R. about 1860. General gunsmith on Canal Street, Palmyra, New York.

Bennett, L. 1859–1868. Shop located at 46 Dorrance Street, Providence, Rhode Island, made percussion rifles and shotguns.

Berdan, Hiram 1866–1871. Commanded a Federal Regiment of Sharpshooters formed in New York city during the Civil War. Invented and patented, January 10, 1865, a breechblock that altered muzzle-loading Springfield percussion rifles to breech-loading.

Berg, A. 1857–1866. General gunsmith at Akron, Ohio.

Berlin, Abraham 1773–1786. Maker of Kentucky flintlock rifles at Easton, Pennsylvania.

Berlin, Isaac 1781–1817. Born 1755, established gunsmithery at Easton, Pennsylvania. Made Kentucky flintlock rifles, active here until 1817, died in 1831.

Bernard, Joseph about 1800. General gunsmith at Walpole, New Hampshire.

Berry, William 1834–1865. Shop located at Poughkeepsie, New York, 1834 to 1840; moved to 6 Daniels Street, Albany, New York, 1840 to 1865. Made J. W. Cochran Patent (December 28, 1858) turret percussion revolvers.

Berstro, J. H. about 1835. Made flintlock rifles at Buffalo, New York.

Bertholf, James about 1845. General gunsmith and dealer at 62 Barclay Street, New York, New York.

Best 1760–1775. Shop at Lancaster, Pennsylvania, made Kentucky flintlock rifles.

Betterlich, F. J. 1867–1875. General gunsmith and dealer at Nashville, Tennessee, name also **Betterlich & Legler** later.

Betz, Andreas 1754–1767. Established a gunsmithery at Wachovia, North Carolina.

Beutter Bros. about 1850. Plant at New Haven, Connecticut. Made percussion match and target rifles.

Bevier, James 1867–1870. Shop at Plymouth, Ohio, maker of percussion hunting rifles and shotguns.

Beyer, N. about 1770. Made Kentucky flintlock rifles at Lebanon, Pennsylvania.

Bicaise, Benjamin 1831–1859. General gunsmith and dealer on State Street, Charleston, South Carolina.

Bickel, Henry about 1800. Flintlock Kentucky rifle maker at York, Pennsylvania.

Bickel, Louis 1878–1883. Maker of percussion hunting and match rifles, shop at Akron, Ohio.

Bicknell, Thomas 1799–1803. Had contract making Model 1795 flintlock muskets for United States Government, shop located in Philadelphia, Pennsylvania.

Biddle, R. & W. C. (Brothers) 1800–1835. Made Kentucky flintlock rifles at Philadelphia, Pennsylvania.

Bideman, Daniel about 1835. General gunsmith at 79 Wood Street, Philadelphia, Pennsylvania.

Bidwell, Oliver 1756–1812. General gunshop at Hartford, Connecticut.

Bielry about 1770. Shop at Philadelphia, Pennsylvania, made heavy dragoon flintlock pistols.

Billinghurst, William 1834–1861. Born Monroe County, New York, 1807. Established a gunshop at 9 Stillson Street, in 1834 and later at 41 Main Street, Rochester, New York. Made heavy hunting and match rifles with false muzzles, also a percussion revolving rifle.

Billups & Hassell 1862–1864. Made percussion rifles and pistols for the Confederate States Government at Mount Prairie, Anderson County, Texas.

Bird, A. N. 1853–1865. General gunsmith located at Kent, Ohio.

Bird, C. & Co. 1790–1830. Plant located at Philadelphia, Pennsylvania, made flintlock pistols and rifles. Name changed to **Bird Bros.**, 1830 to 1857, made percussion pistols.

Bird, John 1858–1898. General gunsmith at Oskaloosa, Iowa.

Birsel, Samuel about 1835. General gunsmith at Germantown Road, Philadelphia, Pennsylvania.

Bisbee, D. H. 1835–1860. Made high-grade percussion hunting and match rifles, shop at Norway, Maine. Known for fine workmanship.

Bischens, Benjamin about 1845. General gunsmith at Carondolet Avenue, St. Louis, Missouri.

Bishop, Henry H. 1846–1857. Located at 32 Exchange Street, Boston, Massachusetts, maker of percussion pistols.

Bishop, William 1818–1850. Made flintlock rifles and smoothbore long guns at 40 Congress Street, Boston, Massachusetts.

Bitterlich, Frank J. about 1855. General gunsmith and dealer at Nashville, Tennessee.

Black, Cenas about 1845. General gunsmith at Walnut Street, St. Louis, Missouri.

Blackwood, Marmaduke 1775–1777.
Armorer and gunsmith for the Pennsylvania Militia at Philadelphia, Pennsylvania. Made flintlock muskets.

Blaisdel, Jonathan about 1775.
Gunsmith at Amesbury, Massachusetts, made flintlock muskets.

Blake, P. & E. W. about 1825. Shop at New Haven, Connecticut, general gunsmith.

Blakley, John & Matthew about 1840. General gunsmith at 44 Sheriff Street, New York, New York.

Blanchard, Thomas 1810–1830.
Made flintlock muskets and fowling pieces, shop at Sutton, Massachusetts.

Blankenship, W. S. about 1880.
General gunsmith at Hot Springs, North Carolina.

Bliss & Goodyear 1866–1887. Made percussion and metallic cartridge revolvers at New Haven, Connecticut, under the W. H. Bliss patents (April 23, 1878).

Blunt & Syms 1837–1865. Partners Orison Blunt and J. G. Syms, plant located at 44 Chatham Street, New York, New York. Made small arms, derringer-type percussion pistols, pepperboxes, percussion and metallic cartridge revolvers.

Blymire, George about 1780. General gunsmith in York County, Pennsylvania.

Broadlear, Samuel about 1795.
Made flintlock muskets at Boston, Massachusetts.

Bobb, Anthony 1778–1781. Shop at Reading, Pennsylvania. Made flintlock Kentucky rifles.

Bolen, F. G. about 1855. Maker of pepperboxes and percussion revolvers at 104 Broadway, New York, New York.

Bolton, Enoch 1660–1665. Gunsmith at Charlestown, Massachusetts Bay Colony.

Boniwitz, John about 1775. Flintlock musket and rifle maker at Lebanon, Pennsylvania.

Bonsall, Samuel about 1770. General gunsmith on Queen Street, Charleston, South Carolina.

Boone, Samuel about 1770. Shop located in Berks County, Pennsylvania, made flintlock Kentucky rifles. Either brother or nephew of Daniel Boone.

Booth, Pomeroy about 1850. General gunsmith on Wadsworth Street, Hartford, Connecticut.

Booth, Richard & William 1797–1820. Shop located at 88 South Second Street, Philadelphia, Pennsylvania, made flintlock holster and cased pairs of dueling pistols. Bought out Richard Constable.

Border, Amos & Daniel (Brothers) 1843–1851. Makers of percussion Kentucky rifles in Bedford Township, Bedford County, Pennsylvania.

Border, Samuel 1825–1861. Shop located in Somerset County, Pennsylvania. Made flintlock and, later, percussion Kentucky and hunting rifles.

Bortree, William about 1830. General gunsmith at 433 North Third Street, Philadelphia, Pennsylvania.

Bosler, Joseph about 1800. General gunsmith at Fourth Street, Philadelphia, Pennsylvania.

Bosworth 1760–1775. Flintlock Kentucky rifle maker at Lancaster, Pennsylvania.

Boteler, John about 1820. General gunsmith in Washington, D. C.

Bourne, William 1862–1865. Made percussion revolvers after the Colt models for the Confederate States Government at Savannah, Georgia.

Bouron, and Son, P. 1861–1880. Gunsmiths and importers of European arms at 534 Chartres Street, New Orleans, Louisiana.

Bovee, George & Theodore 1859–1885. General gunsmiths at Madison, Wisconsin.

Bowen, Andras about 1830. General gunsmith on Charles Street, Providence, Rhode Island.

Bowen, B. B. about 1850. Shop located at Bethel, Vermont, general gunsmith.

Bowers, John E. 1837–1841. General gunsmith at 21 St. Philip Street, Charleston, South Carolina.

Bowers, William about 1840. Shop located at Middlebury, Vermont, general gunsmith.

Bown, James 1810–1848. Flintlock Kentucky rifle maker at Pittsburgh, Pennsylvania. Became **James Bown & Son** at 136 Wood Street, Pittsburgh, 1848 to 1874. Made percussion rifles and pistols.

Boyd, Robert 1772–1778. Made flintlock muskets for New York Militia. Gunshop located at New Windsor, New York.

Boyd, William about 1815. General gunsmith at Harrisburg, Pennsylvania.

Boyer, Daniel & Henry 1790–1810. Flintlock Kentucky rifle makers at Orwigsburg, Pennsylvania.

Boyington, John S. about 1845. Percussion rifle maker at South Coventry, Connecticut.

Bradley, H. about 1850. Shop located at Liverpool, New York, made percussion hunting rifles.

Brammer, George 1795–1820. Gunsmith in Chesapeake County, Ohio, made flintlock Kentucky rifles.

Brand Arms Co. 1870–1880. Plant at Norwich, Connecticut, made metallic cartridge whaling guns.

Brandt, John about 1830. General gunsmith and Pennsylvania flintlock rifle maker at Lancaster, Pennsylvania.

Brant, Jacob about 1855. General gunsmith at 46 St. Clair Street, Pittsburgh, Pennsylvania.

Breck, William about 1845. General gunsmith at 242 Market Street, St. Louis, Missouri.

Breffeil, John about 1830. General gunsmith and dealer at 148 Meeting Street, Charleston, South Carolina.

Brenise, George about 1815. General gunsmith at York, Pennsylvania.

Brey, Elias 1838–1868. Shop located at Pennsburg, Pennsylvania. General gunsmith.

Briggs, William 1849–1859. Percussion Kentucky rifle maker at Norristown, Pennsylvania.

Bright, Jacob about 1820. General gunsmith at Washington, District of Columbia.

Brison, H. M. about 1840. Shop located on Oak Street, St. Louis, Missouri. General gunsmith.

Bristol Firearms Co. 1856–1860. Owned by General A. E. Burnside and George P. Foster. Made Burnside breech-loading percussion carbines under United States Government contract. These carbines were the Burnside patent of March 25, 1856, and the George P. Foster patent of April 10, 1860. About 1000 carbines were made at the plant at Bristol, Rhode Island. The company failed in 1860, and General Burnside assigned his patents to the **Burnside Rifle Company** of Providence, Rhode Island.

Broadlear, Samuel about 1795. Gunsmith at Boston, Massachusetts. Made flintlock muskets.

Brockway, Norman S. 1861–1900. Born 1841, established gunshop at West Brookfield, Massachusetts, 1861–1867. Moved to Bellows Falls, Vermont, 1867 to 1900, made percussion target and match rifles, also hunting rifles. Died in 1906.

Brong, Joseph 1760–1800. Kentucky flintlock rifle maker of excellent workmanship. Shop at Lancaster, Pennsylvania.

Brong, Peter 1795–1816. Shop at North Queen Street, Lancaster, Pennsylvania, made flintlock Kentucky rifle of excellent workmanship and ornate design.

Bronoup, James about 1800. General gunsmith at Philadelphia, Pennsylvania.

Brooke, John about 1845. Shop at Third Street, St. Louis, Missouri. General gunsmith.

Brookes, Richard about 1675. Gunsmith at Boston, Massachusetts Bay Colony.

Brooklyn Arms Co. 1863–1867. Plant at Brooklyn, New York, made metallic cartridge revolvers of the F. P. Slocum patents, dated January 27, 1863.

Brooks, Francis about 1790. Flintlock rifle and pistol maker at 87 Front Street, Philadelphia, Pennsylvania.

Brooks, John about 1805. Flintlock Kentucky rifle maker at Lancaster, Pennsylvania.

Brooks, William F. 1861–1867. Plant located in New York, New York, manufactured the Gibbs breech-loading percussion carbine patented by L. H. Gibbs of New York, January 8, 1856. Under United States Government contract, 1052 carbines were purchased by the Ordnance Board in 1863.

Brown, David about 1840. General gunsmith at Lancaster, Pennsylvania.

Brown, D. B. about 1860. Shop located at Cambridge, Massachusetts.

Brown, George A. about 1845. General gunsmith at 43 Main Street, Rochester, New York.

Brown, H. M. 1838–1842. General gunsmith and dealer at 26 Olive Street, St. Louis, Missouri.

Brown, John 1840–1866. Gunsmith at Fremont, New Jersey, 1840 to 1866. His son, Andrew Brown, carried on the shop from 1866 to 1872.

Brown, Jonas about 1835. General gunsmith at Buffalo, New York.

Brown Manufacturing Company 1869–1873. Plant located at Newburyport, Massachusetts, owner J. H. Brown. Made rifles under the Ballard Patents (November 5, 1861) and metallic cartridge two-barrel derringer-type pistols. This company was the successor to the Merrimac Arms Company.

Brown, S. C. about 1850. General gunsmith at 29 Potter Street, Hartford, Connecticut.

Brown, W. H. about 1835. General gunsmith at 126 Wood Street, Pittsburgh, Pennsylvania.

Brown, William 1850–1871. General gunsmith and dealer at 208 Clay Street, San Francisco, California.

Browning, Jonathan 1825–1879. Born in Tennessee in 1805. Established first gunshop at Nauvoo, Illinois, in 1825. He was active there until 1840, when he moved to Iowa and set up a gunshop about eight miles south of Kanesville, near Council Bluffs, Iowa. Here he developed two types of percussion repeating rifles, one a sliding bar in the breech with five loads and a revolving cylinder of five shots. He moved to Ogden, Utah, in 1851 and was active there until his death in 1879.

His two sons, John Moses Browning, born at Ogden, Utah, in 1855, and Mathew Sandefur Browning, born at Ogden, Utah, in 1859, carried on the business after his death. John M. Browning was an inventive genius, and Mathew S. Browning carried on the production and financial side of the business. J. M. Browning received his first patent in 1879 for a metallic cartridge rifle in which a lever opened the breech, ejected the used cartridge and cocked the piece. This was sold to Winchester Arms Co. In 1880 the name was changed to **Browning Bros.** The first patents for a lever-action repeating metallic cartridge rifle were issued in 1884, and this became known as the famous '89 Model Winchester. Later patents for slide-action repeating rifles and shotguns were sold to Winchester Arms. They received the automatic pistol and machine gun patents on April 20, 1897. Mathew Sandefur Browning died in 1923, and John Moses Browning died in 1926. The present corporate name is **Browning Arms Co.**, St. Louis, Missouri.

Brunner, Joseph about 1845. General gunsmith and dealer at 62 Second Street, St. Louis, Missouri.

Brush, John about 1715. Maker of flintlock muskets at Williamsburg, Virginia.

Bryant, James about 1800. Flintlock Kentucky rifle maker in Lampeter Township, Lancaster County, Pennsylvania.

Bryant, Silas 1818–1821. General gunsmith at Cincinnati, Ohio.

Buchalew, about 1850. Maker of Kentucky percussion rifles at South Rowlesburg, Virginia (now West Virginia).

Buchanan, Jacob about 1795. General gunsmith and dealer at 9 Queen Street, Charleston, South Carolina.

Buchmiller, Robert 1850–1869. Percussion Kentucky rifle maker. Shop located at 43 North Queen Street, Lancaster, Pennsylvania.

Buck, H. A. 1875–1883. Shop located at Chicopee, Massachusetts, prior to 1875, then moved to West Stafford, Connecticut, made breech-loading rifles.

Buckingham, about 1850. Maker of high-grade percussion match or target rifles at Delhi, New York.

Buckley, Anton 1854–1864. Shop located at Cincinnati, Ohio, general gunsmith.

Buckwalter, Abraham, Henry, and John (Brothers) 1771–1780. Makers of flintlock Kentucky rifles, gunsmithery in Lampeter Township, Lancaster County, Pennsylvania.

Buell, Elisha & Enos (Son) 1797–1850. Elisha established a gunshop at Marlborough, Connecticut, in 1797. First government contract for Model 1795 flintlock muskets. Second government contract for Model 1808 flintlock muskets during War of 1812. In 1825 his son, Enos, took over the business and continued until 1850.

Bulow, Charles about 1795. Flintlock Kentucky rifle maker at Lancaster, Pennsylvania.

Bunsen, about 1865. General gunsmith at Belleville, Illinois.

Burger, David about 1785. General gunsmith at 106 Queen Street, Charleston, South Carolina.

Burger & Smith about 1770. General gunsmith on Meeting Street, Charleston, South Carolina.

Burgess, Andrew 1874–1887. Shop located at Owego, New York, made percussion match and hunting rifles.

Burlingame, Ira about 1840. General gunsmith at Woodstock, Vermont.

Burnham, Elisha 1776–1781. Maker of flintlock muskets for Connecticut Militia at Hartford, Connecticut.

Burns, Henry about 1870. General gunsmith at Lewisburg, Ohio.

Burnside Arms Co. 1860–1865. Successor to the **Bristol Firearms Co.**, plant located at Bristol, Connecticut. General A. E. Burnside assigned his patents to the company. Made Burnside breech-loading carbines under United States Government contract for the Civil War. Later moved to Providence, Rhode Island.

Burt, A. M. 1861–1865. Office in New York, New York, plant at Trenton, New Jersey. Had United States Government contract, dated December 26, 1861, for Model 1861 percussion Springfield rifles.

Burt, John about 1770. Maker of flintlock Kentucky rifles at Donegal Township, Lancaster County, Pennsylvania.

Burton, L. 1871–1883. General gunsmith, shop located at Norwalk, Ohio.

Busch, about 1775. Kentucky flintlock rifle maker at Lancaster, Pennsylvania.

Buskell, W. J. about 1845. Made underhammer percussion rifles and pistols at Glens Falls, New York.

Buss, Charles about 1850. Percussion revolver maker at Marlboro, New Hampshire. Cylinder turned by hand. Patented April 25, 1854.

Bussey, J. F. about 1840. General gunsmith at 42 Blackstone Street, Boston, Massachusetts.

Butler, John 1775–1778. Flintlock musket maker at Lancaster, Pennsylvania, for the Pennsylvania Militia.

Butler, Walter E. about 1855. General gunsmith at Haverhill, Massachusetts.

Butner, Herman about 1815. Shop located at Bethania, North Carolina. General gunsmith.

Butterfield, Jesse S. 1851–1865. Established first as **Butterfield & Nippes** in Philadelphia (Kensington), Pennsylvania, from 1851 to 1854, then as **J. S. Butterfield,** 1854 to 1865. Butterfield was the patentee (December 11, 1855) of a disc primer used on percussion revolvers. He had a large stock of Butterfield Revolvers on hand just prior to the outbreak of the Civil War. These were bought by the governors of the southern states and used by the Confederate Armies. Butterfield had Federal Government contracts for his revolvers during the Civil War.

Byrkit, A. H. 1867–1875. Maker of heavy percussion "Plains" rifles at Fairfield, Iowa.

NOTES

Calderwood, William 1807-1819. Maker of flintlock Kentucky rifles and Army Model 1808 flintlock pistols. Shop located on Germantown Road, Philadelphia, Pennsylvania.

Call, George 1775-1780. Shop located at Lancaster, Pennsylvania, made flintlock Kentucky rifles.

Campbell, William about 1780. Made flintlock muskets for the Maryland Militia at Annapolis, Maryland.

Canfield & Bro. about 1855. Located at Baltimore, Maryland, made percussion pepperbox-type pistols.

Carey, J. 1850-1882. General gunsmith in Clinton County, Ohio.

Carey, M. 1857-1869. Maker of percussion hunting and heavy "Plains" rifles, shop located at Lexington, Ohio.

Carey & Co., William H. about 1850. Custom-made percussion shotguns, excellent workmanship. Shop located in New York, New York.

Carleton, Michael about 1830. Maker of percussion rifles at Haverhill, New Hampshire.

Carlile, H. about 1780. Maker of flintlock Kentucky rifles at Lancaster, Pennsylvania.

Carpenter, John 1771-1790. Shop located in Lancaster, Pennsylvania, made flintlock Kentucky rifles.

Carroll, Lawrence 1786-1790. Shop located at Spruce Street, Philadelphia, Pennsylvania. General gunsmith.

Carruth, Adam 1809-1821. Flintlock musket maker for South Carolina Militia, shop located at Greenville, South Carolina, moved to Philadelphia, Pennsylvania, in 1816, active there untill 1821.

Cartwright, John 1840-1865. Maker of percussion match and hunting rifles at Ottawa, Ohio.

Carver, James 1860-1880. Shop located at Pawlet, Vermont, made percussion shotguns and hunting rifles.

Caskell, E. about 1850. General gunsmith, shop at Natchez, Mississippi.

Caswell, Thomas 1812-1836. Made Model 1808 flintlock muskets for New York State Militia, shop located on State Street, Lansingburg, New York. Succeeded by his son, John M. Caswell, who carried on the business until 1836.

Cave, Christopher 1776-1780. Shop located on Dock Street, Philadelphia, Pennsylvania, did general gunsmithing and made flintlock muskets.

Chacon, Paul about 1815. General gunsmith at Concord Street, Baltimore, Maryland.

Chaffee, R. S. 1884-1889. Plant located at Springfield, Massachusetts, made the Chaffee-Reese (R. S. Chaffee-General J. N. Reese Patent, March 30, 1875) bolt-action metallic cartridge magazine rifles.

Chamberlain, E. about 1850. Made percussion pistols at Southbridge, Massachusetts.

Chamberlain, Joseph about 1815. General gunsmith at 13 Lutheran Street, Albany, New York.

Chandler, Stephen about 1775. Armorer and flintlock musket maker for the Connecticut Militia. Shop in Connecticut, exact location not known.

Chapin, Lyman about 1830. General gunsmith at 93 State Street, Rochester, New York.

Chapman, James 1770-1776. Maker of flintlock muskets for the Pennsylvania Militia, shop located in Bucks County, Pennsylvania.

Chapman, Josiah 1771-1778. Shop located at Frederickstown, Maryland, made flintlock muskets for the Maryland Militia.

Charrier, Jacques 1812-1831. Shop located on Market Street, Baltimore, Maryland. Importer of French flintlock pistols, did general gunsmithing.

Chase, Anson 1828-1860. Shop located at Enfield, Massachusetts, 1828 to 1830, moved to Hartford, Connecticut, 1830 to 1834, then to New London, Connecticut, 1834 to 1860.

Chase, William 1854-1870. Made percussion hunting rifles at Pandora, Ohio.

Chatens, Charles about 1810. Made flintlock muskets and pistols at Baltimore, Maryland.

Cherrington, Thomas P., Sr. 1765-1805. Shop located at Cattawissa, Pennsylvania, made flintlock Kentucky rifles and pistols. Cherrington, Sr., died in 1805, and his son, T. P. Cherrington, Jr., carried on the business until 1858.

Chicago Arms Co. 1883-1897. Plant located at Chicago, Illinois, made "Protector" Palm revolvers and standard-type metallic cartridge revolvers.

Chilcote, J. E. 1845-1870. Made heavy percussion rifles at Dry Run, Pennsylvania.

Chipman, Darius 1799-1816. Born in Salisbury, Connecticut, in 1758. Established a gunsmithery at Rutland, Vermont, in 1799 and received a United States Government contract for Model 1795 Army Flintlock Muskets. Moved to New York, New York, in 1816, where he practiced law until he died in 1820.

Chipman, Samuel 1790-1800. Established a shop at Vergennes, Vermont, and received a United States Government contract for Model 1795 Army Flintlock Muskets. Made other flintlock arms. May have been a brother of Darius Chipman.

Chittle, Frederick about 1830. Maker of flintlock rifles and muskets at Buffalo, New York.

Choate, N. M. 1850-1875. Shop located at Auburn, New York, made percussion match rifles.

Chriskey, Lewis about 1815. Shop located at Philadelphia, Pennsylvania, made flintlock Kentucky rifles.

Christ, Daniel and Jacob (Brothers) 1772-1780. Flintlock Kentucky rifle makers at Lancaster, Pennsylvania.

Churchill, Joshia 1864-1866. Shop located at Belle Plain, Minnesota, made heavy percussion rifles.

Churchill, O. 1846-1850. Made percussion pistols, shop located at Albany, New York.

Clagett, Alexander about 1800. Shop located at Hagerstown, Maryland, made under United States Government contract Model 1795 Army Flintlock Muskets.

Clapham, Josiah 1776-1779. Made flintlock muskets for the Virginia Militia. Location in Virginia not known.

Clark, Alvan 1839-1848. Maker of percussion rifles at Cambridge, Massachusetts, 1839 to 1841, moved to Boston, Massachusetts, 1841 to 1848.

Clark, Carlos 1863-1875. Shop located at Manchester, New Hampshire, made percussion hunting rifles.

Clark, Carlos C. 1832–1846. Maker of flintlock and, later, percussion rifles at Windsor, Vermont.

Clark & Co., F. H. about 1870. Plant located at Memphis, Tennessee, made derringer-type percussion pistols.

Clark, John about 1805. Maker of flintlock Kentucky rifles at Reading, Pennsylvania.

Clark, Joseph about 1800. Shop located at Danbury, Connecticut, had United States Government contract for Model 1795 Army Flintlock Muskets.

Clark, Joseph Andre about 1815. Flintlock Kentucky rifle maker at Detroit, Michigan.

Clark, R. S. 1833–1850. Shop located at Albany, New York, made percussion hunting rifles.

Clark & Sneider 1882–1884. Plant located at 214 Pratt Street, Baltimore, Maryland, general arms makers and dealers.

Clark, William 1783–1790. Maker of flintlock pistols, shop at Philadelphia, Pennsylvania.

Clause, Henry about 1820. Flintlock Kentucky rifle maker, Heidelberg Township, Lehigh County, Pennsylvania.

Clippinger, Joseph 1846–1854. General gunsmithing and percussion rifles, shop located at New Carlisle, Ohio.

Coates, James 1810–1814. Shop located at Philadelphia, Pennsylvania, made flintlock pistols.

Cobb, Henry and Nathan (Brothers) 1795–1801. Makers of flintlock muskets at Norwich, Connecticut. Had United States Government contract for Model 1795 Army Flintlock Muskets.

Cochran, John Webster 1837–1876. Patentee (April 29, 1837) of the turret percussion revolvers and rifles, established in New York, New York, 1837 to 1863, moved to New Hamburg, New York, 1863 to 1876. Most of these revolvers and rifles were made by C. B. Allen, Springfield, Massachusetts.

Cochran, Robert about 1835. General gunsmith located at Rose Alley, Philadelphia, Pennsylvania.

Cocklin, Nicholas 1834–1848. General gunsmith, shop located at 24 Catherine Street, New York, New York, 1834 to 1841; 90 Chatham Street, New York, New York, 1841 to 1843; 111 Bowery, New York, New York, 1843–1848.

Cofer, Thomas W. 1861–1875. Made brass frame percussion revolvers after the Whitney model (except that it had a sheath trigger) for the Confederate armies. Located at Portsmouth, Virginia, 1863 to 1865, moved to Norfolk, Virginia, 1865–1875. After the Civil War, made percussion shotguns.

Coffers, Augustus 1848–1857. Made percussion Kentucky rifles, shop located on North Queen Street, Lancaster, Pennsylvania.

Cogswell, S. about 1810. Shop located at Albany, New York, had United States Government contract for Model 1808 Army Flintlock Muskets.

Coldren, Samuel about 1855. Maker of percussion Kentucky rifles at North Queen Street, Lancaster, Pennsylvania.

Collier, Elisha Hayden 1807–1863. Developed a practical flintlock revolver with a revolving cylinder and firing through a single barrel. The cylinder, however, was turned by hand after each chamber was fired. The piece was 14 inches over-all and had a 6⅜-inch octagonal barrel, smoothbore and .47 caliber. He made his models in Boston, Massachusetts, where he had a gunshop, and completed them in 1810. Unable to interest any financial capital in the United States, he took his models to London in 1811 and was granted Patent #74 in the British Patent Office. Sixty flintlock revolvers and twenty-four revolving long arms were fabricated in England. He returned to Boston, Massachusetts, in 1852 and established a gunshop at 88 Elliott Street, where he was active until his death in 1863.

Colt, Samuel 1836–1862. Samuel Colt was born July 19, 1814, at Hartford, Connecticut. His father, Christopher Colt, operated a woolen textile mill. After schooling at Amherst Academy, he shipped on a sailing vessel out of Boston, August 2, 1830, for Calcutta, India. While on this voyage he made a wooden model of a firearm with a revolving breech and firing through a single barrel, which was the forerunner of the Colt Revolver of today.

He was awarded his first United States patent February 25, 1836, and with financial help established a plant at Paterson, New Jersey, under the corporate name of **The Patent Arms Manufacturing Company,** chartered by the New Jersey legislature, March 5, 1836. His first revolvers were produced early in September, 1836, and are now known to collectors as "Colt Patersons." They had octagon barrels, varied in length from 4½ to 12 inches and caliber .28–.31–.34–.36. These pieces had a folding trigger and no trigger guard. The cylinder pin on the early models had a cup-shaped end and was used as a ramrod. These pieces are marked "Patent Arms M'g Co. Paterson N.J. Colts Pt." About 2000 of these revolvers were made from 1836 to 1841.

Colt's first United States Army Ordnance Board test was held at West Point, New York, in June, 1837, but the United States Army did not adopt the revolver at this time. The Ordnance Board reported that "from its complicated character, its liability of accidental discharge, and other reasons this arm is entirely unsuited to the general purposes of the Service." Even without official Army approval, the popularity the Colt revolver acquired among frontiersmen with these first models was never lost. In the Southwest, these revolvers were traded for $200 in gold or silver. However, in February, 1838, Colt sold 50 revolving rifles at $125 each and 12 revolvers to Colonel William S. Harney in Florida, where he was fighting the Seminoles.

In 1840 Colt brought out his second "Paterson" model, the first with the lever ramrod, which made it possible to load without removing the cylinder. The only other change was a slight modification in the shape of the butt. These arms, however, were expensive compared with the percussion single-shot pistol, and sales were limited. Due to internal dissension and financial difficulties, **The Patent Arms Manufacturing Company** became insolvent in 1843 and for 4 years no revolvers were made. General Zachary Taylor, then in action in the Mexican War, demanded revolvers; and in January 1847 the Army Board of Ordnance ordered 1000 revolvers at $28.00 each from Samuel Colt, who had retained his original patent rights. Captain Samuel H. Walker of the Texas Militia suggested to Colt some improvements in design and action; and this revolver was known as the Army Model 1847, and the first model to have a year designation (known to collectors as the "Walker" or "Whitneyville" Colt). These were made at the Eli Whitney Armory at Whitneyville, Connecticut, under Colt's supervision. The specifications of this model were .44 caliber, 6 shots percussion,

15½ inches over-all, a 9-inch round barrel, single-action and improved trigger mechanism, and trigger guard squared at butt end, loading lever same as previous model, weight 4 pounds 9 ounces, butt design very similar to the Colt of today. These were the first Colt arms sufficiently standardized to have interchangeable parts. The barrels were marked "Address Sam'l Colt New York City." (Colt's New York city address was 155 Broadway.) Up to this time, Colt did not stress his military rank of Lieutenant Colonel, which he had held in the Connecticut Militia (Putnam Phalanx) since 1840, as he fully realized that to officers of the regular army this would make it difficult for him on future contracts.

In the Spring of 1848, Colt set up his own plant on Pearl Street, Hartford, Connecticut, and this plant was on a production-line basis. He received his next contract from the government for an Army Revolver Model 1848, known to collectors as the "Colt Dragoon." This was caliber .44, percussion six shots and over-all length 14 inches, barrel 7½ inches, and it weighed 4 pounds. These were stamped on the cylinder either "U. S. Dragoons," "U.S.M.I." (U. S. Mounted Infantry), or "U.S.M.R." (U. S. Mounted Rifles), and marked "Address Sam'l Colt New York City." These were fitted with detachable shoulder stocks and used as carbines. Some of these shoulder stocks were hollow and fitted as a canteen. All Colt revolvers were serially numbered on the various parts of the frame and cylinder. To be of value to collectors, all parts should bear the same serial number. However, the numbers on the extension shoulder stock could not match the number on the revolver, as the stocks were made on separate order for shipping to various United States Arsenals and the Ordnance Department paid no attention to numbers when issuing revolvers and shoulder stocks.

In the latter part of 1848, Colt made his first belt, or pocket, model. This was known as "The Wells Fargo," as that company contracted for these revolvers and used them to arm their messengers. This model was .31 caliber, percussion, five shot, and had no loading lever on the arm. They were made with 3-, 4-, 5- and 6-inch octagon barrels and were marked on top of barrel "Address Sam'l Colt New York City." Colt's revolvers were first nickel-plated at the factory in 1848.

Colt's next model was known as the Pocket Model of 1849, and was a popular arm and made until 1872. This revolver was .31 caliber, had a loading lever, and was chambered first for 5 shots and later for 6 shots. Early models had octagon barrels and were marked "Address Sam'l Colt New York City." Later models had round barrels and were marked "Address Sam'l Colt Hartford, Conn."

In 1850 Colt patented the fluted and semi-fluted cylinders used on all Colt models from that time on. When these revolvers were issued, officers of the Army and Navy received them first, as it considerably lightened the arm without sacrificing the strength of the cylinder.

In the latter part of 1850, Colt received his first contract from the Navy Department, and this revolver was known as the Navy Model 1851, was .36 caliber, 6-shots percussion with octagon barrel. This model had the cylinder engraved with the naval action between the ships "Mississippi" and a Mexican vessel and inscribed "Engaged 16 May 1843." This and later engravings on the cylinder were the design and work of W. L. Ormsby, 116 Fulton Street, New York, New York. Ormsby was a celebrated steel engraver who cut steel roller dies for the stamping. He made other cylinder engravings for Colt: "The Stage Coach Holdup" and "The Battle with the Indians."

Samuel Colt, now realizing the possibility of the English, continental-European, and India markets, on May 1, 1852, established the Colts Patent Repeating Arms Manufactory in Besborough Place, Thames Bank, Pimlico, London. He met considerable opposition from English gunmakers, but developed a successful business and secured some British Government contracts and a Russian Government contract. These were marked "Address Col. Colt London" and had British proofmarks on the frames and cylinders. However, his United States business and the Hartford plant demanded his attention, and in 1857 he closed the London plant. A small company assembled the material on hand under the name of **The London Pistol Company.** All Colt arms made in England were marked on barrel, "Col. Sam'l Colt London," and Colt arms made at Hartford for export to England were marked "L" after the serial number, and "E" designated Europe. Some of the European government contracts stipulated in their contract that serial numbers were to be omitted, and this was done.

In 1855, he acquired property on the Connecticut River at Hartford and built his plant, which is the site of the present plant. Colt's next United States Government contract was secured in 1859 and was for both Army and Navy revolvers. The Army model of 1860 was .44 caliber percussion, 6 shots, ratchet-lever ramrod housed in barrel frame, total length 14 inches, barrel 8 inches. Marked either "Address Sam'l Colt, Hartford Ct." or "Address Col. Sam'l Colt New York U. S. America."

The Navy revolver was Model 1861, .36 caliber, 6 shots ratchet-lever ramrod in barrel housing and a 7½-inch round barrel marked "Address Col. Sam'l Colt New York U. S. America." These two models were extensively used in the War between the States.

The last percussion-cap revolver Colt made was a belt, or pocket, revolver, Model 1862, caliber .36 and 5 shots ratchet-lever ramrod and a groove in recoil shield to place and remove percussion caps.

Samuel Colt died at Hartford, Connecticut on January 10, 1862, and is buried there.

Colton, W. M. about 1850. Maker of percussion rifles at Leominster, Massachusetts.

Columbia Armory 1861–1865. Confederate States Arsenal at Columbia, South Carolina. Made and repaired percussion muzzle-loading rifles. Destroyed by Federal Troops in February 1865.

Columbus Fire Arms Manufacturing Co. 1861–1865. Plant located at Columbus, Georgia, had Confederate States contract for Navy Colt type percussion revolvers.

Colville, Alexander A. about 1820. General gunsmith at Little River, Maine.

Colvin, M. S. about 1870. Made percussion heavy match rifles and shotguns. Shop located at Salamanca, New York.

Colvin, R. I. about 1860. Patented a percussion pepperbox attached to hilt of cavalry saber at Lancaster, Pennsylvania.

Concord Gun Manufactory about 1845. Owned by Cutchins & Crosby. Plant at Concord, New Hampshire, made percussion rifles and shotguns.

Condry, W. P. about 1850. General gunsmith at Portsmouth, Virginia.

Cone, D. D. 1860–1867. Patented and made experimental models of a metallic cartridge revolver at Washington, D. C.

Conestoga Rifle Works about 1780. Made Kentucky flintlock rifles at Lancaster, Pennsylvania.

Conner, William about 1850. General gunsmith at 34 Wentworth Street, Charleston, South Carolina.

Connecticut Arms Co. 1862–1869. Plant located at Norwich, Connecticut. Made Stephen W. Wood Patent, November 18, 1862, teat cartridge revolver.

Connecticut Arms & Mfg. Co. 1866–1869. Made Henry Hammond Patent (January 23, 1866) breech-loading percussion pistols, carbines, and rifles. Plant at Glastonbury, Connecticut.

Constable, Richard 1815–1845. Shop located at 88 South Second Street, Philadelphia, Pennsylvania. Maker of flintlock pistols and fowling pieces and cased flintlock and later percussion dueling pistols of fine workmanship.

Continental Arms Co. 1866–1870. Plant located at Norwich, Connecticut. Made Charles W. Hopkins Patent (May 27, 1862) percussion pepperboxes.

Converse, William H. 1873–1880. General gunsmith at Colorado Springs, Colorado.

Cook & Bro. 1861–1865. Made various types of arms under contract for the Confederate States. Plant at New Orleans, Louisiana, 1861 to 1863, moved to Athens, Georgia, 1863 to 1865.

Cook, E. W. 1850–1861. Made heavy percussion hunting and target rifles at 93 Main Street, Lockport, New York.

Cook, Jacob about 1810. Kentucky flintlock rifle maker, Lancaster County, Pennsylvania.

Cook, William about 1835. General gunsmith at 11 Stone Street, Rochester, New York.

Cookson, John 1701–1762. Gunsmith at Boston, Massachusetts Bay Colony. Made flintlock multi-shot musket of 9 charges, one charge behind the other. John Cookson died 1762, and the shop was carried on by his son, Samuel, and his grandson, John, until 1775.

Coon, Levi, Sr. 1776–1821. Shop located at Ithaca, New York, made flintlock Kentucky rifles, business carried on by his sons, Levi, Jr., and Daniel, into percussion period.

Coons, Joseph about 1810. General gunsmith at Philadelphia, Pennsylvania.

Cooper, B. & J. 1803–1831. Flintlock rifle and pistol makers at 19 Partition Street, New York, New York. Made fine pairs of cased flintlock dueling pistols.

Cooper Fire Arms Mfg. Co. 1851–1863. Plant at Frankfort, Philadelphia, Pennsylvania. Made James Maslin Cooper's patent (March 20, 1860) double-action percussion revolvers under both Army and Navy contracts. Moved to Pittsburgh, Pennsylvania, 1863 to 1869, and made percussion revolvers under the name of **J. M. Cooper.**

Cooper, Henry T. 1845–1858. Located at 177 Broadway, New York, New York, made percussion target rifles and pistols. Became **Cooper & Pond** in 1858.

Cooper, J. R. about 1850. Shop located in New York, New York. Made or imported percussion pepperboxes.

Copeland, T. 1868–1874. Made metallic cartridge revolvers at Worcester, Massachusetts.

Corley, Christopher about 1815. General gunsmith at 352 Water Street, New York, New York.

Corns, Abraham about 1850. Shop located at Lancaster, Pennsylvania, made percussion Kentucky rifles.

Cosmopolitan Arms Co. 1862–1865. Made H. Gross Patent (May 22, 1855) percussion breech-loading carbines under United States Government contract. Plant at Hamilton, Ohio.

Coster, Abraham 1810–1814. Flintlock Kentucky rifle maker in Philadelphia, Pennsylvania.

Coulthard, J. about 1850. Percussion rifle and pistol maker at Natchez, Mississippi.

Coutty, Samuel 1783–1795. Maker of flintlock pistols at Philadelphia, Pennsylvania. Fine workmanship.

Cowell, Ebenezer 1775–1782. Flintlock musket maker at Allentown, Pennsylvania, 1775 to 1779 and at Philadelphia, 1779 to 1782.

Cowell, Joseph 1745–1775. General gunsmith at Boston, Massachusetts Colony.

Cowles & Smith—Cowles & Son 1866–1876. W. W. Cowles made single-shot metallic cartridge pistols as Cowles & Smith, Chicopee Falls, Massachusetts, 1866 to 1871, and as Cowles & Son, Chicopee Falls, Massachusetts, 1871 to 1876.

Cox & Son about 1845. Makers of percussion pistols at Atlanta, Georgia.

Crabb, Thomas 1799–1805. Flintlock Kentucky rifle maker at Frederick Town, Maryland.

Craft, Royal 1799–1810. General gunsmith at Rutland, Vermont.

Craig, Robert 1775–1778. Maker of flintlock muskets at Philadelphia, Pennsylvania.

Craig, William about 1845. Shop located on Sixth Street, Pittsburgh, Pennsylvania, made percussion Kentucky rifles.

Crandall, M. F. about 1850. Made heavy percussion hunting and match rifles at Tonawanda, New York.

Creamer, B. about 1800. Maker of flintlock rifles and pistols at Philadelphia, Pennsylvania.

Crissey, Elias 1854–1874. Shop located at Hooversville, Pennsylvania, did general gunsmithing and made percussion rifles.

Croissant, Martin about 1860. General gunsmith at 204 Washington Street, Albany, New York.

Cromwell, Levi about 1860. General gunsmith at Baltimore, Maryland.

Cromwell, Simon about 1825. Shop located at Edgecomb, Maine, general gunsmith.

Croneberger, A. 1848–1854. Maker of percussion Kentucky rifles at Bucyrus, Ohio.

Crosslay, J. M. about 1850. General gunsmith at Uniontown, Pennsylvania.

Crow, C. A. 1860–1880. Maker of percussion rifles, shop located at Lima, Ohio.

Croysdale, Thomas about 1810. General gunsmith at Baltimore, Maryland.

Cryth, John about 1800. Flintlock Kentucky rifle maker at Lancaster, Pennsylvania.

Cullman, Charles 1850–1874. Maker of heavy "Plains" percussion rifles at Columbus, Ohio.

Cullough, William about 1850. General gunsmith, made percussion rifles at Brookville, Pennsylvania.

Cummings, Charles A. 1866–1871. Plant located at Worcester, Massachusetts, 1866 to 1869, changed to **Cummings & Lane,** Worcester, 1869 to 1871.

Cummings, John about 1840. General gunsmith at 18 Kingsley Street, Hartford, Connecticut.

Cunkle, George about 1840. Percussion Kentucky rifle maker, shop located at Harrisburg, Pennsylvania.

Cunningham, W. A. 1852–1860. General gunsmith at Mt. Vernon, Ohio.

Curry, Charles & Nathaniel (Brothers) 1852–1882. General gunsmith and dealer at 83 Battery Street, San Francisco, California. In 1856, moved to 87 Battery Street; in 1862 to 317 Battery Street. Charles Curry died in 1863, leaving the business to his brothers, Nathaniel and John, and in 1864 the name was changed to **N. Curry & Bro.** at the same address. Charles Curry was the agent for Deringer percussion pistols, and his name was stamped on the barrel as agent from 1856 to 1863. **N. Curry & Bro.** carried on this agency, and their name was stamped on the barrel from 1863 to 1868. In 1869, the firm moved to 113 Sansome Street, San Francisco, California, where they were located until 1882.

Curtain, Joseph about 1840. Shop located at St. Georges Street, St. Louis, Missouri. General gunsmith.

Curtis, Jesse 1776–1780. Flintlock musket maker for the Connecticut Militia at Waterbury, Connecticut.

Cushing, Alvin B. 1829–1843. Shop located at 25 Second Street, Troy, New York, made percussion rifles and pistols.

Cyphers, M. B. 1859–1868. Maker of percussion rifles at Skowhegan, Maine.

NOTES

Daigle, Marcelin about 1870. General gunsmith at Houma, Louisiana.

Dalby, H. C. 1859–1866. Maker of percussion rifles at Berlin, Ohio.

Dallam, Richard 1775–1778. Flintlock musket maker for Maryland Militia in Hartford County, Maryland.

Dana, I. 1777–1780. Made flintlock muskets and rifles at Canton, Massachusetts.

Dance Brothers & Park 1863–1865. Made percussion Army and Navy revolvers of the Colt type for the Confederate forces. Plant at Columbia, Texas, 1863 and 1864, and at Anderson, Texas, 1864 and 1865.

Daniels, H. & C. 1838–1850. Percussion rifle maker at Chester, Connecticut.

Danne, John W. 1860–1867. Maker of percussion rifles for Confederate Army at Mobile, Alabama.

Danner, Jacob 1821–1844. General gunsmith. Made flintlock and, later, percussion Kentucky rifles at Canton, Ohio.

Danseth, Andrew 1800–1805. General gunsmith at Cincinnati, Ohio.

Dantz, H. A. 1874–1878. Shop located at New Haven, Connecticut, did general gunsmithing.

Darling Bros. 1836–1840. Barton and Benjamin M. Darling received a United States patent, dated April 13, 1836, for a single-action percussion pepperbox. They first manufactured at Bellingham and later at Shrewsbury, Massachusetts, then at Woonsocket, Rhode Island. After patent conflicts with Ethan Allen and Samuel Colt, together with manufacturing difficulties, they closed the business in 1840 and stopped making what they called their "Patent Rotary Pistol."

Daub, Jacob about 1800. Flintlock Kentucky rifle maker in Berks County, Pennsylvania.

Davenport, W. H., Firearms Co. 1855–1894. Plant located at Norwich, Connecticut. Made single shot percussion and, later, metallic cartridge rifles.

Davidson, T. & Co. 1850–1860. Made percussion Kentucky rifles at Cincinnati, Ohio.

Davies, William about 1650. General gunsmith at Boston, Massachusetts Bay Colony.

Davis, A. about 1820. Made flintlock Kentucky rifles, shop at Deposit, New York.

Davis & Bozeman 1862–1865. Made percussion rifles for the State of Alabama for Confederate troops. Shop located in Coosa County, Alabama.

Davis, Jarvis about 1845. General gunsmith at Buffalo, New York.

Davis, N. R. 1853–1870. Shop located at Assonett, Massachusetts, made percussion rifles and shotguns. Name changed to **N. R. Davis & Co.** (same location), 1861 to 1870.

Davis, William about 1835. General gunsmith at 91 Beaver Street, New York, New York.

Day, Silas 1831–1850. Located in New York, New York, general gunsmith.

Deashner about 1850. Maker of percussion rifles at Ithaca, New York.

Deberiere, Henri 1769–1774. General gunsmithing and custom-made flintlock pistols at Philadelphia, Pennsylvania.

Dechard, Jacob 1732–1782. Flintlock Kentucky rifle maker, Philadelphia, Pennsylvania, 1732 to 1753, Lancaster, Pennsylvania, 1753 to 1782.

Deeds, H. W. about 1775. Shop located at Reading, Pennsylvania, made flintlock Kentucky rifles.

Defibaugh, Daniel & William (Brothers) about 1845. Percussion Kentucky rifle makers at Providence Township, Bedford County, Pennsylvania.

DeHaven, Peter 1769–1778. Made flintlock muskets for the Pennsylvania Militia at Philadelphia, 1769 to 1776, then moved to Valley Forge, Pennsylvania, 1776 to 1778.

DeHuff, Abraham about 1780. Flintlock Kentucky rifle maker at Lancaster, Pennsylvania.

DeHuff, Henry 1801–1807. Had contracts with State of Pennsylvania for Model 1795 flintlock muskets and State of Virginia for flintlock pistols. Also, made flintlock Kentucky rifles. Shop located at Lancaster, Pennsylvania.

Delaney, Nelson 1840–1872. Shop located in Reading, Pennsylvania, maker of percussion Kentucky rifles.

Dennis, William about 1815. Made flintlock Kentucky rifles. Shop located at Linglestown, near Wilkes-Barre, Pennsylvania.

DeReiner, Michael 1773–1777. Shop located at Lancaster, Pennsylvania, and made flintlock Kentucky rifles. Also, had flintlock musket contract for the Pennsylvania Militia.

Deringer, Henry, Jr. 1806–1868. Born at Easton, Pennsylvania, October 26, 1786. Apprenticed to his father, Henry Deringer, a gunsmith in Richmond, Virginia. Henry Deringer, Jr., set up his own shop at 612 North Front Street, Philadelphia, in 1806,

and later also had a shop on Tamarind Street between Green and Coates streets. His first pieces were flintlock pistols and muskets under United States Government contracts for the Army and various Indian tribes for hunting weapons. Had government contracts for United States flintlock rifle, Models of 1814 and 1817. While making military arms, he did not neglect the civilian market and built up a reputation for flintlock and, later, percussion hunting rifles and cased dueling pistols. In 1831, he developed the percussion pistol of short rifled barrel and heavy caliber which became the prototype of what is known as the "derringer." The longest known Deringer is .54 caliber and 15 inches over-all, and the shortest is .36 caliber and 3¾ inches over all. He was one of the first gunmakers in the U. S. to employ the percussion system of ignition in non-military arms. In 1845, he received a United States Government contract for the Navy boxlock percussion pistol. The Deringer pocket pistol had a large sale in the South, and this market spread to the Pacific Coast during the gold rush years. His pistols were copied, and even his name and trade mark were stamped on the lock plate and breech of the barrel, which brought on the famous lawsuit of Henry Deringer vs. A. J. Plate (San Francisco). Before the suit was finally settled, Henry Deringer died in Philadelphia, Pennsylvania, on February 26, 1868, in his 81st year, and the damages were awarded his estate on the final settlement of the lawsuit.

Derr, John 1810–1844. Flintlock and percussion pistol and rifle maker at Lancaster, Pennsylvania. Received a United States Government contract for Model 1826 Army flintlock pistol.

Desverneys, Anthony 1785–1798. General gunsmithing and flintlock pistols. Shop located at 165 King

Street, later 83 Broad Street, Charleston, South Carolina.

Deterer, Adam 1740–1778. Flintlock Kentucky rifle maker and also flintlock muskets for the Pennsylvania Militia. Shop located at Lancaster, Pennsylvania.

Devane, James 1776–1832. Shop located in New Hanover County, North Carolina, made flintlock muskets for the North Carolina Militia.

Devane, John 1776–1778. Made flintlock muskets for North Carolina Militia, shop located at Wilmington, North Carolina.

Devendorf, Louis about 1850. Made percussion match and hunting rifles at Cedarville, near Newburgh, New York.

Deverson, Richard about 1810. General gunsmith on Silver Street, Boston, Massachusetts.

Dewey, Ebenezer about 1870. Located at Amber, New York, made heavy percussion target rifles.

Dewey, Samuel 1775–1778. Flintlock musket maker for Connecticut Militia at Hebron, Connecticut.

Dewitt 1848–1854. Percussion rifle maker, shop at Wapakoneta, Ohio.

Dewitt, W. P. about 1850. Shop located at Elmira, New York, made percussion hunting rifles.

Dick, Frederick about 1860. General gunsmith on Batavia Street, Buffalo, New York.

Dick, Walter about 1770. General gunsmith on Meeting Street, Charleston, South Carolina.

Dickert, Jacob 1762–1822. Born Maintz, Germany, January 9, 1740, came to America in 1748, apprenticed to gunsmiths in Lancaster, Pennsylvania, in 1758. Established his own shop in 1762 at Lancaster, Pennsylvania. Flintlock Kentucky rifle maker and had United States Government contract for flintlock muskets and, later, flintlock rifles. Died February 27, 1822.

Dickinson, J. & L. 1863–1880. Plant located at Springfield, Massachusetts. Made mostly metallic cartridge pistols and revolvers.

Dickson, Nelson & Co. 1861–1865. William Dickson and O. O. Nelson had contract with Confederate States Government for percussion rifles and carbines. Fabricated originally at Dickson, Alabama, then at Rome, Georgia, then Adairsville, Georgia, and finally at Dawson, Georgia.

Dickey, David about 1780. General gunsmith and flintlock Kentucky rifle maker in Middletown Township, Cumberland County, Pennsylvania.

Diemer, I. about 1870. Made heavy percussion target rifles at Taunton, Massachusetts.

Diettrich, J. F. 1840–1860. Maker of heavy percussion "Plains" rifles at St. Louis, Missouri.

Diffenderfer, John & Michael (Brothers) about 1780. Flintlock Kentucky rifle makers in Earl Township, Lancaster County, Pennsylvania.

Dimick, Horace E. 1849–1874. One of the pioneer gunmakers of the western frontier. Born in Vermont, migrated West and, in 1849, established a gunshop at 38 Main Street, St. Louis, Missouri. St. Louis was a good gun market and outfitting town for the Plains at that time, and Dimick made heavy percussion "Plains" rifles and carried a stock of percussion revolvers and derringers. In 1860, the name was changed to **H. E. Dimick & Co.** and located at 42 North Main Street, St. Louis, Missouri, at which time he employed 26 gunsmiths. Dimick died in 1874.

Dingler, J. about 1810. Flintlock Kentucky rifle maker at Easton, Pennsylvania.

Dittrich, J. P. 1862–1865. Made percussion muskets for the Confederate Army at Mobile, Alabama.

Dodd, John 1755–1762. General gunsmith, made fine flintlock pistols. Shop located on Meeting Street, Charleston, South Carolina.

Dodds, James 1863–1886. General gunsmith, made percussion rifles at Xenia, Ohio, 1863 to 1866, and at Dayton, Ohio, 1866 to 1886.

Dodge, Grover about 1840. General gunsmith at Woodstock, Vermont.

Dogarthy, George about 1805. Shop located at 246 King Street, Charleston, South Carolina, did general gunsmithing.

Doherty, J. about 1870. Maker of percussion rifles at Petersburg, Virginia.

Dohrmann, Frederick about 1840. General gunsmith at 53 First Street, St. Louis, Missouri.

Doll, Jacob 1780–1805. Flintlock Kentucky rifle maker, also had contract for Model 1795 flintlock muskets for Pennsylvania Militia. Shop at York, Pennsylvania.

Donn & Bro., James 1880–1884. General gunsmiths at Canton, Ohio.

Dougherty, Absalom about 1840. Percussion Kentucky rifle maker in Annville Township, Lebanon County, Pennsylvania.

Douglass, John about 1840. Shop located at Huntington, Pennsylvania, made percussion Kentucky rifles.

Dow, Eli S. 1859–1880. General gunsmith at Dayton, Ohio.

Downing, L. about 1840. Shop located at 50 Congress Street, Troy, New York. General gunsmith.

Draton, John 1770–1775. General gunsmith on Tradd Street, Charleston, South Carolina.

Drepperd, The House of, 1777–1870. Justus Drepperd (Drebbert) of Malines, Holland, emigrated to America, arrived in Philadelphia on October 23, 1752. In 1753 he settled in Lancaster, Pennsylvania, and married Dorothea Bibbert, and their first child, a son, was born in 1756 and christened John Michael.

In 1775, John Michael Drepperd joined Colonel Mathias Slaugh's Battalion of Pennsylvania Riflemen and saw action in the Revolutionary War. He returned to Lancaster, Pennsylvania, in 1777 and set up a gunsmithery making Kentucky rifles. This first gunshop was in a linen-weaving mill inherited from his father. The Drepperd name was carried on by his sons, nephews, and grandsons for over three-quarters of a century.

The earliest known Drepperd Rifle is dated 1778. From that date on, Drepperd Rifles and Pistols were made in increasing numbers, and by 1825 ten members of the Drepperd family were interested, either financially or as makers of firearms. Most of these rifles and pistols were marked only "Drepperd," with no initials of the maker.

Col. Eifort of Greenup, Kentucky, was a Drepperd agent. Some members of the Drepperd family migrated to Indiana, Illinois, and Missouri Territories to service Drepperd arms. With this effort Drepperd arms moved westward with the pioneers. Out of the Drepperd gunshops came many apprentices who later made their names as Kentucky rifle makers.

The Drepperds known to have been active in gun or gunlock making were: Christian, born 1761; Jacob, born 1766; Jacob, born 1782; John, born 1784; George, born 1787; John, born 1803; Henry, born 1803; William, born 1816; Michael, born 1818.

Dreyac, A. about 1815. General gunsmith at 36 Laight Street, Baltimore, Maryland.

Dufort, Augustus 1855–1861. General gunsmith and importer of cased percussion dueling pistols, located on King Street, Charleston, South Carolina.

Dull, Jacob about 1800. Flintlock Kentucky rifle maker at Lancaster, Pennsylvania.

Dunkle, George about 1825. Shop located at Sheppensburg, Cumberland County, Pennsylvania, made flintlock Kentucky rifles.

Dunlap, H. C. 1848–1854. General gunsmith at Kossuth, Ohio.

Dunseth, Andrew about 1800. Shop located at Cincinnati, Ohio; general gunsmith.

Dunwicke, William 1770–1776. Maker of flintlock muskets for the Pennsylvania Militia in Chester County, Pennsylvania.

Duprez, S. about 1870. General gunsmith at Del Norte, Colorado.

Durr, Christian about 1700. General gunsmith at Lancaster, Pennsylvania.

Dutton, John S. 1856–1868. Made heavy percussion match or target rifles, shop at Jaffrey, New Hampshire.

Dwight, H. D. about 1845. General gunsmith shop at Belchertown, Massachusetts.

NOTES

Eagle Firearms Co. 1865–1870. Office located at 262 Broadway, New York, New York, and factory at Rock Falls, New York (J. J. Marlin Co.). Made Plant Patent cartridge revolvers. Cartridge loaded from the front of cylinder.

Eagle Mfg. Co. 1862–1866. Plant at Norwich, Connecticut, made percussion Springfield rifles under United States Government contract, dated December 26, 1861.

Eagle Rifle Works 1833–1851. Made percussion Kentucky rifles at Philadelphia, Pennsylvania.

Ealer, Lewis 1848–1857. Shop at Lancaster, Pennsylvania, made percussion Kentucky rifles.

Earle, Thomas 1767–1810. Born August 27, 1737, established a gunshop at Leicester, Massachusetts, in 1767. Made flintlock muskets and fowling pieces of fine workmanship. Died March 21, 1819.

Earle, Elias 1811–1816. Shop at Centerville, North Carolina; had United States Government contract, dated February 16, 1815, for flintlock muskets.

Earley, Amos about 1860. General gunsmith at West Hanover, Pennsylvania.

Early, Jacob 1864–1886. Born in Tennessee in 1816. Served in United States Army as Ordnance gunsmith, 1853 to 1860. Established gunshop at Atcheson, Kansas, in 1864, made heavy percussion rifles. Active until his death 1886.

Eastman, J. I. 1863–1868. Shop located at Concord, New Hampshire. Made percussion rifles and single-shot underhammer pistols.

Eastman, Robert about 1830. General gunsmith at Brunswick, Maine.

Eaton, J. 1838–1874. Shop located at Concord, New Hampshire; made percussion pistols, pepperboxes and shotguns.

Eaton & Kittridge about 1850. General gunsmiths and percussion rifle makers at 236 Main Street, Cincinnati, Ohio.

Eberle, A. 1855–1863. Shop located at 545 Vine Street, Cincinnati, Ohio; general gunsmith.

Eberman, Henry about 1820. Made flintlock Kentucky rifles at Lancaster, Pennsylvania.

Eberly, John 1774–1777. Shop located at Lancaster, Pennsylvania, made flintlock muskets for the Pennsylvania Militia.

Eckart Bros. 1857–1869. Henry and William Eckart had a general gunsmithery at St. Joseph, Missouri.

Eckel, Charles 1855–1860. General gunsmith at Cincinnati, Ohio.

Eddy, James about 1810. General gunsmith at Philadelphia, Pennsylvania.

Edgerton, H. S. about 1855. Maker of percussion rifles, shop at Chenango, New York.

Edmanson, Jacob about 1770. General gunsmith at Broad Street, Charleston, South Carolina.

Edwards & Goodrich 1840–1845. Had United States Government contract for Model 1835 Springfield flintlock muskets, dated January 8, 1840. Plant at New Haven, Connecticut.

Eggers, Samuel 1840–1865. Made heavy percussion whale guns at New Bedford, Massachusetts.

Eicholtz, H. C. 1866–1875. Shop located at 58 North Queen Street, Lancaster, Pennsylvania. General gunsmith.

Eicholtz, Robert L. 1848–1857. Made percussion Kentucky rifles. Shop located on Lime Street, Lancaster, Pennsylvania.

Eickhorn, Christopher about 1845. General gunsmith at 1 Huron Street, Cleveland, Ohio.

Eldridge, W. H. about 1860. Percussion rifle maker at Rushford, New York.

Elgin, George 1836–1839. Designed the Elgin Cutlass Pistol at New York, New York. Made by Morrill, Mossman and Blair, Amherst, Massachusetts, and C. B. Allen, Springfield, Massachusetts.

Eller, H. O. about 1870. Made heavy percussion target and hunting rifles at Cairo, Illinois.

Elliot, W. H. 1863–1872. General gunsmith and dealer at 404 Broadway, New York, New York.

Elliott, Matthew & Nathan about 1800. Had United States Government contract for Model 1795 flintlock muskets; shop located at Kent, Connecticut.

Ellis, J. A. about 1855. Made percussion rifles and shotguns at Canandaigua, New York.

Ellis, Ruben 1808–1829. General gunsmith at Albany, New York.

Ellis, Willard C. 1865–1870. Made single-shot metallic cartridge pistols at Springfield, Massachusetts.

Ells, Josiah 1854–1857. Had patent dated August 1, 1854, for percussion revolvers. Shop located at Pittsburgh, Pennsylvania.

Elton, Thomas about 1780. General gunsmith at Philadelphia, Pennsylvania.

Elwell, H. about 1770. Flintlock Kentucky rifle maker at Liverpool, Pennsylvania.

Ely, A. F. 1848–1860. General gunsmith at Mt. Vernon, Ohio.

Ely, Martin 1770–1776. Made flintlock muskets for Massachusetts Militia at Springfield, Massachusetts.

Emery, N. 1859–1865. General gunsmith at Chatfield, Minnesota.

Emmes, Nathaniel 1789–1805. General gunsmith at Fifth Street, Boston, Massachusetts, 1789 to 1805. Nathaniel Emmes, Jr., carried on the business at 23 Fish Street, Boston, Massachusetts, 1805 to 1816.

Englehart, J. 1830–1840. Percussion Kentucky rifle maker, also percussion pepperboxes, at Nazareth, Pennsylvania.

English, J. about 1835. Shop at Philadelphia, Pennsylvania. General gunsmith.

Erichson, G. about 1855. General gunsmith and dealer at Houston, Texas.

Ernst, J. 1780–1820. Flintlock Kentucky rifle maker at Frederick, Maryland.

Escherich, Anton, Ferdinand & Francis (Brothers) about 1860. Made percussion pistols and rifles and did general gunsmithing. Fine workmanship. Shop located at 477 West Baltimore Street, Baltimore, Maryland.

Eshelman, John about 1840. Maker of percussion Kentucky rifles at Lancaster, Pennsylvania.

Estabrook, J. M. about 1860. Made percussion rifles at Milford, Massachusetts.

Estabrook, William about 1870. General gunsmith at Armada, Michigan.

Evans, Brooke 1821–1825. Had United States Government contract for flintlock pistols and Model 1808 flintlock muskets. Located at Evansburg near Valley Forge, Pennsylvania.

Evans, Edward & James (Brothers) 1801–1818. Shop located at Evansburg near Valley Forge, Pennsylvania. Made under United States Government contract, Model 1795 flintlock muskets.

Evans, Freman about 1850. General gunsmith at Portland, Maine.

Evans, J. E. 1850–1865. Made percussion derringer-type pistols and long-barrel percussion pistols. Shop located at 25 North Second Street (1850 to 1855), and 86 South Street (1855 to 1865), Philadelphia, Pennsylvania.

Evans, Owen & Edward 1790–1815. Had United States Government contract for Model 1808 flintlock muskets and pistols. Shop located at Evansburg near Valley Forge, Pennsylvania.

Evans, Stephen 1742–1797. Gunsmith at Mt. Joy Forge near Valley Forge, Pennsylvania, and the founder of the family of gunsmiths bearing his name.

Evans, William L. 1823–1833. Made Model 1826 Army and Navy flintlock pistols under United States Government contract at Evansburg near Valley Forge, Pennsylvania.

Evans Rifle Mfg. Co. 1868–1880. Made Warren R. Evans patent (September 19, 1871) repeating metallic cartridge rifles and carbines. Plant at Mechanic Falls, Maine.

Evatt, Edward 1804–1818. General gunsmith at 35 Laight Street, Baltimore, Maryland.

Evatt, Columbus about 1840. Located in Baltimore, Maryland. General gunsmith.

NOTES

Fair, James about 1870. General gunsmith at Dayton, Ohio.

Fairbanks, A. B. 1827–1841. Flintlock pistol maker and, later, percussion pistols and derringers, at Boston, Massachusetts.

Fales, James 1859–1868. General gunsmith at New Bedford, Massachusetts.

Falley, Richard 1761–1808. Born Georges River, Maine, January 31, 1740. Established a gunsmithery at Westfield, Massachusetts, in 1761. Served as a captain at the Battle of Bunker Hill and through the Revolutionary War. After the war, reestablished the gunsmithery at Westfield, Massachusetts, and received a United States Government contract for Model 1795 flintlock muskets. Was armorer for Massachusetts Militia and later Superintendent of Springfield (Massachusetts) Armory. Died at Westfield, Massachusetts, September 3, 1808.

Fancher, Thomas 1770–1779. Maker of flintlock muskets for the Connecticut Militia. Shop at Waterbury, Connecticut.

Farnot, Frederick, Frank & Jacob 1775–1783. Flintlock Kentucky rifle makers at Lancaster, Pennsylvania.

Farrington, William B. 1855–1864. General gunsmith and percussion rifle maker at Concord, New Hampshire.

Farrow, William B. 1878–1885. Shop located at Holyoke, Massachusetts, made percussion match rifles.

Farver, William 1848–1854. Made percussion Kentucky rifles. Shop located in Brown County, Ohio.

Faulk, Adam about 1775. Flintlock Kentucky rifle maker at Lancaster, Pennsylvania.

Faust, Joseph H. 1844–1888. Made percussion Kentucky rifles and did general gunsmithing at Alsace, Pennsylvania.

Favier, Peter A. about 1845. General gunsmith at 67 West Pratt Street, Baltimore, Maryland.

Fay, Edward about 1830. Shop located at 7 Beaver Street, Albany, New York. General gunsmith and made percussion Kentucky rifles.

Fayetteville Armory 1840–1865. One of the United States Government southern arsenals was established at Fayetteville, North Carolina. At the time of the secession of North Carolina from the Union in 1861, this was taken over by the State and contained a considerable stock of percussion muskets and rifles and other military supplies. The Confederate States operated the armory during the Civil War, making percussion rifles. The buildings were destroyed by General Sherman in March, 1865.

Fehr, J. 1830–1835. Flintlock Kentucky rifle maker at Nazareth, Pennsylvania.

Fere, Joll 1853–1869. Probably grandson or grandnephew of Jacob Ferree (having simplified the spelling of the name), maker of percussion Kentucky rifles at Cumberland, Ohio.

Ferree, Jacob 1774–1807. Born of French Huguenot ancestors at Lancaster, Pennsylvania, on August 8, 1750, and established a gunsmithery there in 1774, making flintlock Kentucky rifles. In 1784 he moved to Peters Creek, Jefferson Township, Allegheny County, Pennsylvania, and established a powder mill and gunsmithery. He had two sons: Joll, born January 26, 1771, and Isaac, born January 9, 1776, both working with him.

Joll Ferree was armorer of the First

Pennsylvania Regiment at the Battle of New Orleans and died in 1815. Isaac Ferree, who died in 1822, had two sons, Joll Thornton and George Spencer, who carried on the business at Peters Creek, Allegheny County, Pennsylvania, until 1840.

Ferris, George H. 1850–1875. Shop at 9 John Street, Utica, New York, made target or match percussion rifles of fine workmanship.

Fesig, Conrad 1779–1790. Made flintlock Kentucky rifles at Reading, Pennsylvania.

Field, I. about 1790. General gunsmith at Philadelphia, Pennsylvania, made flintlock Kentucky rifles.

Fighthorn, Andrew 1780–1792. Shop located at Reading, Pennsylvania, made flintlock Kentucky rifles.

Finch, Joseph 1800–1828. General gunsmith at 26 Robinson Street, New York, New York, 1800 to 1802, then moved to 54 Vesey Street, New York, 1802 to 1828.

Fischer, Gustave 1860–1864. Maker of percussion target rifles at New York, New York.

Fish, Daniel 1844–1848. General gunsmith at 168 West Broadway, New York, New York.

Fishburn, Philip 1776–1795. Flintlock musket and rifle maker in Dauphin County, Pennsylvania.

Fishel, Jacob 1846–1861. Percussion Kentucky rifle maker. Shop located in Hopewell Township, Bedford County, Pennsylvania.

Fisher, F. G. about 1875. General gunsmith at Greeley, Colorado.

Fisher, Homer 1859–1875. Made heavy caliber percussion rifles at New York, New York.

Fisher, James about 1815. Shop located at 8 Calvert Street, Baltimore, Maryland. General gunsmith.

Fisher, John about 1845. General gunsmith at 195 Greenwich Street, New York, New York.

Fitch, John 1769–1796. Born in 1743, established a gunsmithery on King Street, Trenton, New Jersey Colony in 1769, where he was active until the British Army burned his shop in 1776. He moved to Bucks County, Pennsylvania, in 1777 and operated a gunshop until 1788. During part of this time, he was a lieutenant in General Washington's Army, probably an armorer. He returned to Trenton, New Jersey, in 1788, rebuilt his gunsmith shop on King Street, and was active until 1796 when he moved to Bardstown, Kentucky, where he died in 1798.

Flager, John about 1835. General gunsmith at 51 Diamond Street, Pittsburgh, Pennsylvania.

Flagg & Co., B. 1849–1852. Had United States Government contract for Model 1841 percussion muskets. Shop at Millbury, Massachusetts.

Fleeger, John & William (Son) 1831–1877. Shop located at Federal Street, Allegheny, Pennsylvania. Also known as Allegheny Gun Works. Made percussion Kentucky rifles.

Flohr & Wendell about 1860. General gunshop and dealer at San Francisco, California.

Flowers, Charles 1841–1860. Shop located at Harmony, Pennsylvania. General gunsmith.

Floyd, Thomas about 1770. Gunsmith located on Church Street, Charleston, South Carolina.

Fogarty, V. 1866–1869. General gunsmith at Cambridgeport, Massachusetts.

Fogg, Gilman B. 1845–1870. Maker of percussion rifles and shotguns at 40 Elm Street, Manchester, New Hampshire.

Fogle, Heinrich about 1855. Made percussion Kentucky rifles at Lancaster, Pennsylvania.

Foher, Ludwig about 1775. Maker of flintlock muskets for the Pennsylvania Militia at Philadelphia, Pennsylvania.

Folger, William H. 1846–1854. General gunsmith at Barnesville, Ohio.

Folk, William 1865–1890. General gunsmith at Bryan, Ohio.

Follecht 1740–1770. Maker of flintlock Kentucky rifles at Lancaster, Pennsylvania.

Folsom Arms Co., H. & D. about 1860. Manufacturers and dealers of firearms, some marked with their name, located at 314 Broadway, New York, New York.

Folsom Bros. 1860–1875. General gunsmiths located at 65 St. Charles Street, New Orleans, Louisiana, and later at 9 Decatur Street, New Orleans, Louisiana.

Folsom, Charles 1862–1875. Gunsmith and dealer at 53 Chambers Street, New York, New York.

Folsom & Co., Henry 1853–1870. Located at St. Louis, Missouri, general gunsmith and dealer in all types of firearms.

Foltz, George about 1820. Shop located at Salem, North Carolina, general gunsmith.

Foncannon, M. B. 1848–1855. General gunsmith at Columbus, Ohio, 1848 to 1849, then moved to New Lexington, Ohio, 1849 to 1855.

Fondersmith, George about 1800. Maker of flintlock Kentucky rifles in Strasburg Township, Lancaster County, Pennsylvania.

Fondersmith, John, Sr. & Jr. 1749–1802. Shop located in Strasburg Township, Lancaster County, Pennsylvania. Made flintlock Kentucky rifles and flintlock muskets for the Pennsylvania Militia during the Revolutionary War. Later had United States Government contract for Model 1795 flintlock muskets.

Fondersmith, Luis about 1805. Made flintlock Kentucky rifles in Strasburg Township, Lancaster County, Pennsylvania.

Fondersmith, Samuel G. 1847–1854. General gunsmith and percussion Kentucky rifles at Mason, Ohio.

Fonshill, John 1800–1819. Shop located on Union Street, Baltimore, Maryland, 1800 to 1816 and on North Street, Baltimore, Maryland, 1816 to 1819. General gunsmith.

Forbes, Gilbert 1767–1776. General gunsmith and importer of fine flintlock pistols and fowling pieces. Shop located at present site of 18 Broadway, New York, New York.

Forbes, John W. about 1850. Percussion rifle maker on Highland Street, Worcester, Massachusetts.

Forbes, Nathaniel about 1805. General gunsmith at Plymouth, New Hampshire.

Ford, David 1862–1865. Made percussion Kentucky rifles at Abbeyville, Ohio.

Ford, John 1800–1817. Shop located at Harrisburg, Pennsylvania, made flintlock Kentucky rifles.

Fordney, C. 1800–1830. Made flintlock Kentucky rifles at Cumberland, Maryland.

Fordney, Jacob 1837–1857. General gunsmith at North Prince Street, Lancaster, Pennsylvania.

Fordney, Melchoir 1823–1843. Flintlock Kentucky rifle maker at Lancaster, Pennsylvania. Fine craftsmanship.

Forehand & Wadsworth 1871–1880. Sullivan Forehand and Henry C. Wadsworth were sons-in-law of Ethan Allen and worked with him. In 1871, the name Ethan Allen & Co. at Worcester, Massachusetts, was changed to **Forehand and Wadsworth** and in 1880 to **Forehand Arms Co.**, Worcester, Massachusetts, until 1902, when they closed the business. The companies made metallic cartridge derringer-type pistols and metallic cartridge revolvers of various calibers.

Forker, I. 1859–1866. General gunsmith at Ravenna, Ohio.

Forker, William 1859–1875. Shop located at Meadville, Pennsylvania. General gunsmith.

Forrest, Casper about 1855. General gunsmith at Lancaster, Pennsylvania.

Fortune, Thomas L. 1850–1862. Pioneer gunsmith. Shop located at Mt. Pleasant, Atchison County, Kansas.

Foster, George P. 1849–1865. Plant located at Taunton, Massachusetts, and Bristol, Rhode Island, from 1849 to 1855, then moved to Providence, Rhode Island, 1855 to 1865. Made heavy "Plains" percussion rifles, also Porter Patent rifles and Howard Patent (October 28, 1862) breech-loading carbines.

Foster, W. 1848–1869. Percussion rifle maker. Shop located at Columbus, Ohio.

Foulke, Adam 1773–1794. Made flintlock rifles for the Pennsylvania Militia, also flintlock Kentucky type pistols. Shop at Allentown, Pennsylvania.

Foulks, William about 1775. General gunsmith and flintlock Kentucky rifle maker at Lancaster, Pennsylvania.

Fowler, B. 1835–1850. Maker of percussion pistols at Hartford, Connecticut.

Fowler, D. about 1835. General gunsmith at Shrewsbury, Massachusetts.

Fox, H. A. about 1845. General gunsmith at 8 Sixth Avenue, New York, New York.

Fox, Horace about 1850. Made percussion rifles at Fredensburg, Pennsylvania.

Frailey, Andrew about 1855. Maker of percussion Kentucky rifles. Shop located at Lancaster, Pennsylvania.

France, J. A. about 1860. Shop located at Cobleskill, New York. Made percussion target pistols.

Franck, about 1775. Made flintlock Kentucky rifles at Lancaster, Pennsylvania.

Frazier, John 1740–1756. Born in Scotland and emigrated to the Colonies. Established a gunsmithery at Lancaster, Pennsylvania, in 1740. In 1750, moved to Venango County, Pennsylvania, and was active until 1756.

Frederick, John 1859–1879. General gunsmith at Gouglarsville, Pennsylvania.

Freeman, A. T. 1862–1864. Supervised the manufacture of his patent (December 9, 1862) percussion revolver at Hoards Armory, Watertown, New York.

French, Thomas 1799–1820. Shop located at Canton, Massachusetts. General gunsmith, and had United States Government contract for Model 1808 flintlock muskets and Dragoon flintlock pistols.

Freund, C. 1873–1882. General gunsmith and dealer at Cheyenne, Wyoming.

Frey, Martin about 1800. Maker of flintlock Kentucky rifles at York, Pennsylvania.

Frickey, Samuel about 1800. General gunsmith on Charlotte Street, New York, New York.

Friend, Gabriel about 1760. General gunsmith in Frederick County, Maryland.

Frisbee, J. 1848–1854. Shop located at Cork, Ohio. General gunsmith.

Frontfield, John about 1800. Flintlock Kentucky rifle maker in Providence Township, Montgomery County, Pennsylvania.

Frost, Gideon about 1775. Made flintlock muskets for the Massachusetts Militia. Shop location not known. Also armorer for Massachusetts Regiments.

Fry, Francis about 1855. Early pioneer gunsmith. Shop located in Doniphan County, Kansas.

Fuller, E. T. 1858–1867. General gunsmith at St. Clair, Michigan.

Furby, George 1860–1868. Made percussion rifles and did general gunsmithing at Waterford, Vermont.

NOTES

Gafford, John about 1815. General gunsmith at Cumberland Street, Baltimore, Maryland.

Galbraith, James about 1790. Flintlock pistol maker in Philadelphia, Pennsylvania.

Gall, John about 1850. Shop located at Lancaster, Pennsylvania. Made percussion Kentucky rifles.

Gallagher, Mahlon J. 1860–1865. Patentee of the Gallagher percussion and, later, metallic cartridge breechloading carbine. These were manufactured under his supervision at the Richardson and Overman plant at Philadelphia, Pennsylvania.

Gallatin, Albert 1796–1808. Had United States Government contract for Model 1795 flintlock muskets. Shop in Fayette County, Pennsylvania, 1796 to 1804; moved to Clarksburg, Virginia, 1804 to 1808.

Gander, Peter about 1780. Shop located at Lancaster, Pennsylvania, made flintlock Kentucky rifles.

Gardner, Charles 1844–1855. General gunsmith at 14 North St. Paul Street, Rochester, New York.

Gardner, G. 1859–1865. Shop located at Lima, Ohio. General gunsmith.

Gardner, John 1866–1888. General gunsmith at Columbus, Ohio.

Garret, Herman about 1675. Established gunsmithery at Boston, Massachusetts Bay Colony.

Gaspard, about 1775. Flintlock Kentucky rifle maker at Lancaster, Pennsylvania.

Gautec, Peter about 1780. Shop located at Lancaster, Pennsylvania. General gunsmith.

Geary, William about 1830. General gunsmith on Washington Street, Philadelphia, Pennsylvania.

Geddy, David & William about 1750. Made flintlock pistols and fowling pieces and did general gunsmithing at Williamsburg, Virginia.

Geddy, James about 1730. General gunsmith at Williamsburg, Virginia.

Gelbke, F. L. 1859–1875. General gunsmith and dealer at 14 Dauphin Street, Mobile, Alabama.

Gemmer, John P. 1855–1890. Born in Germany in 1835, emigrated to the United States in 1855 and established a gunshop at Boonville, Missouri, in 1860 moved to St. Louis, Missouri, and was employed by Hawken. Bought the Hawken business in 1862 and continued to make the Hawken type of percussion "Plains" rifle using the Hawken name. In 1870 moved from Washington Street to 600 North Third Street, St. Louis, Missouri.

Gemmill, George about 1850. General gunsmith at Troy, New York.

Genner, Elijah about 1835. General gunsmith. Shop located on Hill Street, Rochester, New York.

Gentz, Peter about 1845. Shop located at 8 Union Lane, Cleveland, Ohio. General gunsmith.

George, Isaac about 1835. General gunsmith at North Fitzhugh Street, Rochester, New York.

George, Jacob about 1800. Flintlock Kentucky rifle maker at Greenwich Township, Berks County, Pennsylvania.

George, S. J. about 1830. General gunsmith at Monterey, Pennsylvania.

Georgia Armory 1862–1864. A Confederate arsenal established at Milledgeville, Georgia, after Georgia seceded from the Union. Made percussion rifles. Destroyed by Federal troops in November 1864.

Gerhart, Daniel 1873–1898. Made percussion match and target rifles of fine workmanship at Reading, Pennsylvania.

German, Christian about 1835. Made percussion rifles and did general gunsmithery. Shop located on Washington Street, Rochester, New York.

Gerrish, John about 1710. General gunsmith at Boston, Massachusetts Bay Colony.

Getz, John 1773–1782. Flintlock Kentucky rifle maker at Lancaster, Pennsylvania.

Ghriskey, Lewis 1812–1816. Flintlock rifle maker at Philadelphia, Pennsylvania.

Gibbs, Abraham 1847–1857. Shop located at 22 Prince Street, Lancaster, Pennsylvania. Percussion Kentucky rifle maker.

Gibbs, Henry 1824–1857. Flintlock and later percussion Kentucky rifle maker at Lancaster, Pennsylvania.

Gibbs, John about 1825. Shop located at Honesdale, Pennsylvania, made flintlock Kentucky rifles.

Gibbs, L. H. 1856–1865. Patented a percussion carbine in New York, New York, on January 8, 1856. These were made for Federal troops during the Civil War by William F. Brooks of New York, New York.

Gibbs & Tiffany 1820–1850. Made percussion pistols of fine quality and presentation pairs of pistols at Sturbridge, Massachusetts.

Gifford, Joseph about 1820. General gunsmith at 70 Market Street, Baltimore, Maryland.

Gilbert, Daniel 1782–1813. Born 1729. Served as a captain in the Revolutionary War. Established a gunshop and forge at Brookfield, Massachusetts, in 1782 and had a United States Government contract for Model 1795 flintlock muskets and later Model 1808 flintlock muskets. Died in 1824 at age 95.

Gilbert, W. about 1835. General gunsmith at Rochester, New York.

Gilchrist, Richard about 1840. Shop located at 50 Congress Street, Troy, New York. General gunsmith.

Gill, Benjamin 1830–1850. Born 1790. Set up a gunshop at Lancaster, Pennsylvania, in 1830, was active about 20 years. Made flintlock and, later, percussion Kentucky rifles. Died 1860.

Gill, Jacob 1820–1831. General gunsmith, made flintlock Kentucky rifles at Lancaster, Pennsylvania.

Gillem, William about 1840. Percussion rifle maker at Jackson, Ohio.

Gilman, Daniel about 1780. Shop located at Maytown, Lancaster County, Pennsylvania. Made flintlock Kentucky rifles.

Gingerich, Henry, 1775–1777. Made flintlock muskets for the Pennsylvania Militia at Lancaster, Pennsylvania.

Glass, Daniel 1848–1859. Shop located at Wyomissing Creek, Berks County, Pennsylvania. Made percussion Kentucky rifles.

Glassbrener, H. about 1800. General gunsmith at Lancaster, Pennsylvania.

Glassick, F. 1840–1865. Maker of percussion pistols, shop located at Memphis, Tennessee.

Glaze & Co., William 1852–1865. Had United States Government contract for percussion pistols, muskets, and rifles. Shop located at Columbia, South Carolina. At the time of the Civil War, the plant was taken over by the Confederacy and called the Palmento Armory. The buildings were destroyed by Federal troops in 1865.

Glazier, John about 1820. Pioneer gunsmith at Belleville, Indiana. Made flintlock Kentucky rifles.

Godfrey, Charles 1885–1890. Gunsmith and dealer at 7 Warren Street, New York, New York.

Godfrey, James about 1840. General gunsmith. Shop located at 81 Market Street, New York, New York.

Godshall, Nicholas about 1765. Flintlock Kentucky rifle maker at Reading, Pennsylvania.

Godwin, Thomas about 1860. Shop located at Portsmouth, Virginia. Made a 9-shot percussion revolver which was not successful.

Goetz, Frederick 1806–1812. General gunsmith on North Second Street, Philadelphia, Pennsylvania. Made flintlock rifles and muskets. In 1808 he took as a partner Charles W. Westphall, and the name became **Goetz & Westphall.** The firm received a United States Government contract for Model 1808 flintlock muskets.

Golcher, James 1820–1833. Flintlock Kentucky rifle maker at Philadelphia, Pennsylvania.

Golcher, John about 1775. Gunsmith at Easton, Pennsylvania. Made flintlock Kentucky rifles.

Golcher, Joseph about 1800. Made flintlock Kentucky rifles and pistols at Philadelphia, Pennsylvania.

Golcher, Thomas 1868–1875. General gunsmith at Philadelphia, Pennsylvania.

Golcher & Simpson 1854–1870. General gunsmith and maker of percussion rifles. William Golcher had the partnership with Simpson from 1854 to 1858 on North Third Street, St. Paul, Minnesota. The partnership was dissolved and became **Wm. Golcher & Co.,** 1858 to 1870.

Gonter, John about 1820. Maker of flintlock Kentucky rifles. Shop located on Penn Street, Reading, Pennsylvania.

Gonter, Peter, Sr. & Peter, Jr. 1750–1818. Flintlock Kentucky rifle makers at Lancaster, Pennsylvania. The father active from 1750 to 1778 and the son active 1778 to 1818.

Gonyea, John about 1815. General gunsmith at 5 Capitol Street, Albany, New York.

Goodling, Peter about 1790. Maker of flintlock Kentucky rifles at York, Pennsylvania.

Goodwin, Jonathan about 1778. Made flintlock muskets for the Connecticut Militia at Lebanon, Connecticut.

Gorsuch, J. M. about 1860. Shop located at Mt. Pleasant, Ohio. Made fine grade of percussion half-stocked rifles.

Goth, F. 1859–1868. General gunsmith at Portland, Maine.

Goubie, Benjamin 1863–1875. Shop located at 12 Dauphin Street, Mobile, Alabama. General gunsmith.

Goucher, Thomas 1774–1777. Made flintlock muskets for the Pennsylvania Militia. Shop located on Market Street, Philadelphia, Pennsylvania.

Goulcher, Emanuel about 1830. Flintlock Kentucky rifle maker on Eighth Street, Philadelphia, Pennsylvania.

Gould, Theodore P. about 1860. General gunsmith at First Street, Niagara Falls, New York.

Gove, Carlos 1876–1885. Made heavy percussion "Plains" rifles at 21 Edmund Street, Denver, Colorado.

Gowdy, James about 1800. General gunsmith on King Street, Charleston, South Carolina.

Graeff, John 1795–1803. Shop located at Lancaster, Pennsylvania, made Model 1795 flintlock muskets for the Pennsylvania Militia.

Graeff, William 1751–1784. Flintlock Kentucky rifle maker at Reading, Pennsylvania.

Grant, John about 1810. General gunsmith at Baltimore, Maryland.

Grant, Samuel about 1800. Had United States Government contract for Model 1795 flintlock muskets. Shop located at Walpole, New Hampshire.

Grant, William N. 1854–1868. General gunsmith at Greenfield, Massachusetts.

Gratiot Mfg. Co. about 1860. Plant located at St. Louis, Missouri. Made .44 caliber Army type percussion revolver.

Grave, John 1769–1773. Flintlock Kentucky rifle maker at Lancaster, Pennsylvania.

Graves, Asa W. about 1845. General gunsmith at West Killingly, Connecticut.

Graves, J. about 1860. Made percussion rifles at Bangor, Maine.

Gray, G. B. about 1865. General gunsmith at Mt. Vernon, Ohio.

Gray, J. B. 1829–1836. Shop located at Fredericksburg, Virginia. General gunsmith.

Great Western Gun Works 1865–1890. Owned by John H. Johnston and his son James H. Johnston. Plant located at 179 Smithfield Street, Pittsburgh, Pennsylvania. Made percussion and, later, metallic cartridge revolvers.

Green & Alling 1871–1879. General gunsmiths at 3 West Main Street, Rochester, New York, 1871 to 1876. Name changed to **Charles Green** at same address, 1876 to 1879.

Green, Samuel about 1840. Shop located at 50 Congress Street, Troy, New York. General gunsmith.

Greene, J. D. 1854–1865. Lt. Col. J. Durrell Greene, United States Army, patented January 3, 1854, a breechloading percussion rifle and carbine. These were first made at Millbury, Massachusetts. In 1865 the **Greene Rifle Works** was established at Worcester, Massachusetts, where the patented rifles and carbines were made under United States Government contract until 1867.

Greenwood & Gray 1862–1865. Eldridge S. Greenwood and William C. Gray had a percussion rifle contract with the Confederate States Government. Plant located at Columbus, Georgia.

Gregory, Richard about 1730. Established a gunsmithery at Boston, Massachusetts Bay Colony.

Gresheim, J. 1775–1783. Maker of flintlock Kentucky rifles at Lancaster, Pennsylvania.

Griffith, Joseph about 1870. General gunsmith and percussion rifle maker at Louisville, Kentucky.

Griffith, Robert E. about 1820. Shop located in Philadelphia, Pennsylvania. General gunsmith.

Griffiths, John 1839–1865. Maker of flintlock and, later, percussion Kentucky rifles at Cincinnati, Ohio.

Grillet, Alexander about 1865. Shop located at Bridesburg, Pennsylvania. Made percussion breech-loading rifles.

Grim, Frederick about 1855. Percussion Kentucky rifle maker at Lancaster, Pennsylvania.

Griswold & Grier 1862–1864. Giles C. Griswold and his brother-in-law, Col. E. T. Grier, established a percussion revolver plant in the Griswold Cotton Gin Company's plant at Griswoldville (near Macon), Georgia. They received a contract from the Confederate Government to make Army and Navy percussion revolvers after the Colt models. Most of these were made with a brass frame. The plant went in operation in June 1862 and was destroyed by Kilpatrick's Federal Cavalry on November 20, 1864.

Griswold, Jesse 1837–1844. General gunsmith in Chambers County, Alabama.

Groff, John about 1795. Flintlock Kentucky rifle maker at Lancaster, Pennsylvania.

Groot, Henry 1866–1871. General gunsmith at Pittsfield, Massachusetts, 1866 to 1868. Migrated to Minneapolis, Minnesota, and active there 1868 to 1871.

Gross, Henry & Charles B. (son) 1841–1886. Henry Gross active at Tiffin, Ohio, 1841 to 1852. His son with him from 1852 to 1875, when the father died and the business was carried on under the name of **Charles B. Gross,** 1875 to 1886. Made the Gross Patent percussion and, later, metallic cartridge revolvers. Henry Gross patented a breech-loading percussion carbine, December 3, 1861, and these were made under United States Government contract during the Civil War.

Grove, Samuel 1779–1783. General gunsmith and flintlock Kentucky rifle maker in York County, Pennsylvania.

Grubb, George about 1800. General gunsmith and dealer. Shop located at 6 Broad Street, New York, New York.

Grubb, Joseph C. 1855–1886. Shop located at 712 Market Street, Philadelphia, Pennsylvania. General gunsmith and dealer.

Grubb, Thomas 1800–1820. Flintlock pistol maker at Philadelphia, Pennsylvania, specializing in cased pairs. Fine workmanship.

Grubb, Tobias about 1820. Flintlock Kentucky rifle maker in Northampton Township, Lehigh County, Pennsylvania.

Grueby, George about 1845. General gunsmith at Portland, Maine.

Guest, John 1776–1808. Operated gunsmithery known as Warwick Foundry near Lancaster, Pennsylvania. Had United States Government contract for flintlock pistols and rifles. Some of the locks on his arms bear Drepperd name.

Guillam, Benjamin about 1775. Made flintlock muskets for the Massachusetts Militia. Location of gunsmithery not known.

Gulliver, Frederick 1845–1850. General gunsmith at 70 Center Street, Cleveland, Ohio.

Guion, T. F. about 1855. Shop located at New Orleans, Louisiana. General gunsmith and dealer.

Gump, Andrew about 1840. Percussion Kentucky rifle maker at Lancaster, Pennsylvania.

Gump, Christian about 1800. Shop located at Lancaster, Pennsylvania. Maker of flintlock Kentucky rifles.

Gump, Jonathan 1849–1870. Maker of percussion Kentucky rifles at Sandusky, Ohio.

Gumpf, Christopher & Christopher, Jr. 1791–1842. Made flintlock and, later, percussion Kentucky rifles at Lancaster, Pennsylvania.

Gumpf, Henry about 1820. Shop located at Lancaster, Pennsylvania, made flintlock Kentucky rifles.

Gumpf, Jacob 1820–1828. Flintlock Kentucky rifle maker at Lancaster, Pennsylvania.

Gumpf, John about 1820. Shop located at Lancaster, Pennsylvania, maker of flintlock Kentucky rifles.

Gumpf, Mathias 1819–1858. Maker of flintlock and, later, percussion rifles. Shop located on Walnut Street, Lancaster, Pennsylvania.

Gumpf, Michael about 1840. Gunsmith at Lancaster, Pennsylvania, made percussion Kentucky rifles.

Gumster, Hiram about 1850. General gunsmith at 101 North Salina Street, Syracuse, New York.

Gunn, William 1790–1813. General gunsmith on Queen Street, Charleston, South Carolina.

Gwyn & Campbell 1861–1865. Edwin Gwyn and A. C. Campbell patented a breech-loading percussion carbine. Patent dated October 21, 1862. Received United States Government contracts for this carbine, which was known as the "Union." Production was in their plant at Hamilton, Ohio.

NOTES

Haag, Christ 1849–1867. Percussion Kentucky rifle maker at Pomeroy, Ohio.

Haberstro, Joseph 1832–1844. General gunsmith and percussion rifle maker. Shop located at 145 North Main Street, Buffalo, New York.

Hackney, William W. 1859–1880. Shop located at Dayton, Ohio. Made heavy caliber percussion "Buffalo" rifles and hunting rifles.

Hadden, James about 1770. General gunsmith in Philadelphia, Pennsylvania.

Haeffer, Jacob 1802–1821. Had United States Government contract for Model 1795 flintlock muskets at Lancaster, Pennsylvania.

Hafer, John about 1820. General gunsmith. Shop located on Liberty Street, Pittsburgh, Pennsylvania.

Haga, Jesse 1848–1854. Shop located in Clinton County, Ohio. Did general gunsmithing and made percussion Kentucky rifles.

Haga, Wolfgang 1767–1790. Flintlock Kentucky rifle maker at Reading, Pennsylvania.

Hager, Jonathan about 1760. General gunsmith in Washington County, Maryland.

Hahn, W. about 1855. General gunsmith in New York, New York.

Haiman & Bro. 1862–1865. Louis and Elias Haiman signed, on August 26, 1862, a contract with the Confederate War Department for Colt Navy-type percussion revolvers. Their plant was at Franklin and Oglethorpe Streets, Columbus, Georgia, and these revolvers were marked, "Columbus Fire Arms Manuf Co Columbus." Federal troops destroyed the building in 1865.

Haines, Isaac 1730–1775. Flintlock Kentucky rifle maker in Lampeter Township, Lancaster County, Pennsylvania Colony.

Halburn, Casper about 1775. Made flintlock muskets for the Pennsylvania Militia at Lancaster, Pennsylvania.

Haldeman, F. about 1800. Shop located in Heidelberg Township, Pennsylvania. General gunsmith, made flintlock pistols.

Hale, H. J. 1840–1852. Made percussion pistols at Worcester, Massachusetts.

Halerstroth, L. 1866–1868. General gunsmith at Fremont, Ohio.

Hall, Alexander 1845–1856. Shop located in New York, New York; general gunsmith.

Hall, Charles 1873–1880. General gunsmith at Lancaster, Pennsylvania.

Hall, Elias about 1850. Shop located at Montpelier, Vermont; general gunsmith.

Hall, H. 1862–1875. General gunsmith at Green Bay, Wisconsin.

Hall, John Harris 1811–1841. Colonel John H. Hall of Yarmouth, Maine, received his first patent for the Hall flintlock breech-loading rifle and carbine on March 21, 1811. From 1811 to 1813 he made his models and some rifles at Portland, Maine. In 1813, he established the **Hall Rifle Works** at Harpers Ferry (then Virginia) and made the rifles with interchangeable parts. In 1815, he received his first United States Government contract and was appointed Asistant Armorer at the Harpers Ferry Government Armory to develop and supervise the making of machinery for the manufacture of his flintlock breech-loading rifle patent. The Hall rifle was first issued to United States troops in 1816 as an experimental arm and were the first breechloaders to be officially adopted by any of the armies of the world. In 1824, the first thousand had been made with interchangeable parts. They were made as flintlock until 1831 and percussion after that date. Col. John H. Hall died February 26, 1841. Under United States Government contract, Simeon North at Middletown, Connecticut, made a number of percussion carbines with the Hall Patent and North's improvement of the patent.

Hall, Perry 1848–1854. Made heavy percussion target and hunting rifles at Ashtabula, Ohio.

Hall, Samuel 1831–1851. Shop located at 118 Fulton Street, New York, New York. Made percussion pistols.

Hall, Samuel about 1775. Made flintlock muskets for the Connecticut Militia at East Haddam, Connecticut.

Hamilton, James about 1800. Made flintlock Kentucky rifles in Fawn Township, York County, Pennsylvania.

Hammond, E. K. about 1850. General gunsmith at West Derby, Vermont.

Hammond, H. 1864–1867. Made percussion carbines and metallic cartridge pistols at Naubuc, Connecticut.

Hampton, John N. about 1835. Flintlock Kentucky rifle maker in West Hanover Township, Dauphin County, Pennsylvania.

Hanatter, Jacob about 1840. General gunsmith in Allen Township, Cumberland County, Pennsylvania.

Hankins, William about 1855. Shop located in Philadelphia, Pennsylvania. General gunsmith.

Hanks, Uriah about 1775. Maker of flintlock muskets for the Connecticut Militia at Mansfield, Connecticut.

Hanni, H. about 1820. General gunsmith at Reading, Pennsylvania.

Hapgood, Joel 1848–1856. Shop located at 30 Washington Street, Boston, Massachusetts. General gunsmithing and percussion rifles and shotguns.

Hapolt, Benjamin & J. H. (Son) 1850–1861. Made cased percussion dueling pistols and did general gunsmithing. Shop located at 45 State Street, Charleston, South Carolina.

Harder, F. 1868–1875. General gunsmith at Green Bay, Wisconsin.

Harder, Jacob 1844–1874. Active at Athens, Pennsylvania, 1844 to 1860. Moved to Lock Haven, Pennsylvania, 1860 to 1874. Made percussion rifles and pistols and cased dueling pistols.

Harder, J. E. 1873–1887. General gunsmith at Clearfield, Pennsylvania.

Hardesty, Charles 1870–1876. Shop located at Los Animas, Colorado. General gunsmith.

Hardinger, Peter about 1780. Flintlock Kentucky rifle maker in Berks County, Pennsylvania.

Hardwicke & Schenkle about 1855. General gunsmiths and dealers at 57 Elm Street, Boston, Massachusetts.

Harmon, Jonas 1847–1854. Shop located at Sulphur Springs, Ohio. General gunsmith work.

Harpers Ferry Armory (United States Arsenal) 1796–1861. In 1794, President Washington was authorized by Congress to establish two Federal armories. The President selected the site of Harpers Ferry, then Virginia, (became West Virginia in 1866) and Springfield, Massachusetts. The armory started operations in 1796 and flintlock muskets, rifles, and pistols were made. These are identified by the markings, "Harpers Ferry" and the year. The earliest known arm so marked is 1801. In 1859, John Brown attempted to seize the Armory and its stock of arms. In 1861, the Armory was burned by its commandant to prevent falling in the hands of the Confederate forces.

Harrington, H. B. about 1850. Made percussion rifles at Lebanon, New Hampshire.

Harrington, Henry 1834–1841. Patented a multi-shot, long arm similar to the pepperbox type at Southbridge, Massachusetts.

Harrington, Luke about 1830. General gunsmith at Sutton, Massachusetts.

Harrington & Richardson 1874–to date. Gilbert H. Harrington and William A. Richardson established the original plant on Herman Street, Worcester, Massachusetts. Made shotguns and metallic cartridge revolvers.

Harrington, Thomas 1853–1860. General gunsmith in Philadelphia, Pennsylvania.

Harris, C. C. about 1880. General gunsmith and dealer at Georgetown, Washington, District of Columbia.

Harris, Edwin S. 1867–1876. Shop located at 177 Broadway, New York, New York. General gunsmith and dealer.

Harris, Henry, 1779–1783. Flintlock Kentucky rifle maker at Lancaster, Pennsylvania.

Harris, Isaac 1772–1776. Maker of flintlock muskets for the Maryland Militia at Savage Town, Maryland.

Harris, John about 1800. Shop located at York, Pennsylvania, made flintlock Kentucky rifles.

Hart, Aaron about 1810. Maker of flintlock Kentucky rifles and flintlock fowling pieces. Shop on Wood Street, Pittsburgh, Pennsylvania.

Hart & Brothers, B. F. 1855–1870. Made percussion pistols and copied Colt model percussion revolvers until stopped by lawsuit. Also dealers in New York, New York.

Hartig, J. 1862–1868. General gunsmith at Dubuque, Iowa.

Hartley & Graham 1880–1890. Shop located at 17 Maiden Lane, New York, New York. General gunsmiths and dealers.

Harwood, Nathaniel 1825–1840. General gunsmith at Brookfield, Massachusetts.

Hasdell, T. R. about 1880. Shop located at 70 East Madison Street, Chicago, Illinois. General gunsmith and dealer.

Haslett, James 1803–1827. Maker of flintlock pistols and pairs of dueling pistols of fine workmanship at 28 Water Street, Baltimore, Maryland.

Hasselmeyer, Charles about 1850. General gunsmith and dealer at 120 Delancy Street, New York, New York.

Hatch, J. about 1845. General gunsmith at Burlington, Vermont.

Hatch, Warren about 1850. Shop located at Plattsburgh, New York. General gunsmith.

Hatfield, about 1840. General gunsmith at Owensburg, Indiana.

Hattersley, Henry 1846–1855. Made percussion rifles and did general gunsmithing at 40 Union Street, Cleveland, Ohio.

Haven, M. about 1800. General gunsmith at Putnam Corners, Ulster County, New York.

Haviland, Frederick about 1835. Shop located at Waterville, Maine; general gunsmith.

Hawk, Nicholas about 1805. Flintlock Kentucky rifle maker at Gilbert, Pennsylvania.

Hawes, Milo about 1850. General gunsmith at Madison, Wisconsin.

Hawken, Henry 1785–1820. Famous pioneer gunsmith and father of two sons who made the name well-known for "Plains" and "Buffalo" percussion rifles. Henry Hawken established a gunsmithery at Lancaster, Pennsylvania, 1785 to 1787. He moved to Hagerstown, Maryland, 1787 to 1808, when he again moved West to St. Louis, Missouri Territory, where he was active until his death in 1820. His eldest son Jacob, born 1786, worked under him and carried on the business at 214 North Main Street, St. Louis, Missouri. In 1822, the younger son, Samuel T., born 1792, joined Jacob, changing the name to J. & S. Hawken, and they were active at this address until 1832, when they moved to 33 Washington Avenue, St. Louis, Missouri. At this time, they had over 30 gunsmiths working for them. Jacob Hawken died in 1849. In 1862, Samuel T. Hawken sold the business to John P. Gemmer, one of his gunsmiths.

Hawker, W. 1859–1868. General gunsmith at Water Street, Saginaw, Michigan.

Hawkins, Henry about 1770. Maker of flintlock Kentucky rifles at Donegal Township, Lancaster County, Pennsylvania.

Hawkins, John about 1685. Established a gunsmithery at Charleston, Carolina Colony.

Hayward, R. B. about 1840. General gunsmith at Montpelier, Vermont.

Heckert, Philip 1769–1799. Flintlock Kentucky rifle maker in York County, Pennsylvania.

Heckman, John about 1830. General gunsmith at 18 Cherry Street, Philadelphia, Pennsylvania.

Heiser, Louis 1857–1866. Percussion rifle maker. Shop located on Washington Street, Tiffin, Ohio.

Heiss, Philip about 1840. General gunsmith at 191 North First Street, St. Louis, Missouri.

Hellinghaus, Frederick 1840–1847. Shop located at 73 Morgan Street, St. Louis, Missouri. General gunsmith.

Hellinghaus, H. about 1855. General gunsmith at San Francisco, California.

Hemenway, Levi 1859–1868. Shop located at Shrewsbury, Massachusetts. General gunsmith.

Hench, Peter 1740–1775. Made flintlock Kentucky rifles at Lancaster, Pennsylvania.

Henderson, Daniel about 1800. General gunsmith at 24 Queen Street, Charleston, South Carolina.

Hendrick, M. S. 1869–1875. Shop located at Amora, Illinois. General gunsmith.

Henkel, Daniel 1807–1817. Shop located at Philadelphia, Pennsylvania. Maker of flintlock Kentucky rifles and had United States Government contract for Model 1808 flintlock muskets.

Henon, Thomas about 1800. General gunsmith on Queen Street, Charleston, South Carolina.

Henry, B. Tyler 1860–1866. Inventor and patentee (October 16, 1860) of the

Henry lever-action rifle at New Haven, Connecticut. This was later the breech and magazine action of the Winchester rifle.

Henry, Stephen 1859–1868. General gunsmith at 167 High Street, Providence, Rhode Island.

Henry, William 1745–1786. Founder of the Henry dynasty of gunsmiths was born May 9, 1729, and established a gunsmithery on Center Square, Lancaster, Pennsylvania, 1745 to 1786, making flintlock Kentucky rifles and pistols. In 1755, he was armorer to the Pennsylvania Regiment in the Braddock Expedition. His son, William Henry, Jr., established a gunsmithery at Nazareth, Pensylvania, and was active 1778 to 1808. His second son, Abraham Henry, active at Lancaster, Pennsylvania, 1798 to 1828, had contract for flintlock muskets for the Pennsylvania Militia. The second son of William Henry, Jr., was John Joseph Henry, who was active in Philadelphia, Pennsylvania, 1801 to 1836. His son, James Henry, was active with his father under the name of **J. Henry & Son** at Third and Noble Streets, Philadelphia, Pennsylvania, 1801 to 1825, and at Boulton, Pennsylvania, 1825 to 1836. When his father, John Joseph Henry, died, the name became the **Boulton Arms Works.**

Hepburn, L. L. 1875–1880. Maker of heavy match rifles at Colton, Vermont.

Herbert, C. H. about 1840. Shop located at Albany, New York. Made saw-handle percussion pistols.

Herfurth, August 1860–1870. Made heavy caliber percussion rifles at Madison, Wisconsin.

Herman, Peter 1864–1871. General gunsmith at Lancaster, Pennsylvania.

Herring, Richard about 1776. Made flintlock muskets for the North Carolina Militia at Wilmington, North Carolina.

Hess, Jacob 1852–1860. Maker of percussion Kentucky rifles. Shop located in Stark County, Ohio.

Hess, Philip about 1830. Shop located in Saegerstown, Pennsylvania. Made flintlock Kentucky rifles.

Hess, Samuel about 1770. Maker of flintlock Kentucky rifles in Matrick Township, Lancaster County, Pennsylvania.

Hetrick, John 1858–1870. General gunsmith at Third Street, Newark, Ohio.

Hidden, Enoch about 1820. Shop located at 293 Cherry Street, New York, New York. General gunsmith.

Hill, Thomas 1790–1810. General gunsmith at Carlotta, Vermont.

Hill, William about 1835. Shop located at Commercial Street, Buffalo, New York. General gunsmith.

Hillegas, Henry 1857–1875. General gunsmith at Harrisburg, Pennsylvania.

Hillegas, J. 1810–1830. Flintlock Kentucky rifle maker at Pottsville, Pennsylvania.

Hilliard, D. H. 1842–1877. Maker of percussion underhammer pistols, rifles and shotguns at Cornish, New Hampshire. He was active 1842 to 1877, and his son, George C. Hilliard, carried on the business from 1877 to 1880.

Hills, Medad 1755–1761. Maker of flintlock muskets and fowling pieces at Goshen, Connecticut Colony.

Hinds, John about 1745. Established a gunsmithery at Boston, Massachusetts Colony.

Hingle, John about 1840. General gunsmith on Walnut Street, St. Louis, Missouri.

Hinkle, George about 1855. Percussion Kentucky rifle maker at Lancaster, Pennsylvania.

Hirth, August 1855–1860. General gunsmith and percussion rifle maker at Pittsburgh, Pennsylvania.

Hoak, Matthias about 1800. Flintlock Kentucky rifle maker at Lancaster, Pennsylvania.

Hoard's Armory 1861–1868. Established by C. B. Hoard at Watertown, New York. Had United States Government contract for Model 1861 percussion rifles, also made A. T. Freeman's Patent (December 9, 1862) Army percussion revolvers.

Hobrecker, John about 1805. General gunsmith at 91 King Street, Charleston, South Carolina.

Hockley, James 1769–1771. Flintlock musket maker in Chester County, Pennsylvania.

Hodgkins & Son 1855–1865. D. C. Hodgkins and his son, Walter C. Hodgkins, had a gunshop at Macon, Georgia. On June 7, 1862, they received a contract from the Confederate States Government to alter flintlock carbines and musketoons held in Confederate Army stores to percussion. They also continued to make percussion rifles for the Confederate forces during the Civil War.

Hoff, Peter about 1860. General gunsmith at Hanover, Pennsylvania.

Hoffman, Christian about 1830. Shop located at 14 Charlotte Street, Philadelphia, Pennsylvania. General gunsmith.

Hoffman, J. V. 1858–1868. Percussion rifle maker at Attica, Indiana.

Hoffman, Louis about 1855. General gunsmith and dealer at Vicksburg, Mississippi. Made derringer-type percussion pistols.

Hogan, John B. 1858–1870. Made percussion pistols and rifles at North Adams, Massachusetts.

Hogy, John 1859–1867. General gunsmith at Bay City, Michigan.

Holbrook, Milton about 1840. Shop located at Rochester, New York. General gunsmith.

Holden, Alexander 1845–1878. General gunsmith at Marseilles, Wyandotte County, Ohio.

Holden, Cyrus B. 1861–1868. Made metallic cartridge rifles at Worcester, Massachusetts.

Holland, W. A. about 1850. Shop located at Boston, Massachusetts; made percussion pistols.

Hollenback, William about 1820. General gunsmith at Washington, District of Columbia.

Hollingsworth, Henry 1773–1780. Made flintlock muskets for the Maryland Militia at Elkton, Maryland.

Hollingsworth, John 1855–1863. General gunsmith at Zanesville, Ohio.

Holmes, George H. 1860–1870. Made fine grade percussion hunting rifles at Defiance, Ohio.

Holmes, John V. 1837–1852. General gunsmith and dealer at 68 Queen Street, Charleston, South Carolina.

Holmes, Richard about 1860. Made heavy caliber percussion rifles at Oswego, New York.

Holt, Judson 1852–1882. Born in New York State 1827, migrated to Michigan in 1852 and established a shop about 2 miles south of Howell,

Michigan. Did general gunsmithing and made percussion rifles, shotguns, and pistols. Died at Howell, Michigan, March 22, 1908.

Holt, Peter about 1855. Made percussion hunting rifles at Ashtabula, Ohio.

Holtry, Joseph 1845–1852. Percussion Kentucky rifle maker at Wyomissing Creek, Berks County, Pennsylvania.

Holtzworth, William about 1820. Shop located at Lancaster, Pennsylvania. General gunsmithing and flintlock Kentucky rifles.

Home, S. 1799–1802. Flintlock musket maker at Stevensburg, Virginia.

Hood Fire Arms Co. 1875–1880. Plant located at Norwich, Connecticut. Made the Freeman W. Hood patent (February 23, 1875) metallic cartridge revolver.

Hood & Foncannon 1848–1853. H. G. Hood and M. B. Foncannon established a gunshop at Columbus, Ohio. This partnership only lasted about a year and the name became **H. G. Hood,** 1849 to 1853. General gunsmithing.

Hooghkirk, Gerret about 1830. General gunsmith at Albany, New York.

Hooker, Thomas 1798–1802. Had United States Government contract to make Model 1795 flintlock muskets. Shop located at Rutland, Vermont.

Hopkins & Allen 1868–1915. Plant located at Norwich, Connecticut. Made metallic cartridge rifles under their own patents, and revolvers under the Merwin and Hulbert patents. Sold to Marlin-Rockwell in 1915.

Horn, Conrad & William (Brothers) 1820–1850. General gunsmiths at Hazelton, Pennsylvania.

Horn, Stephen 1770–1780. Flintlock Kentucky rifle maker at Easton, Pennsylvania.

Horstman & Sons, W. H. 1858–1866. General gunsmiths and dealers at Fifth and Cherry Streets, Philadelphia, Pennsylvania.

Horton, William about 1800. Shop located at 30 Moore Street, New York, New York. General gunsmith.

Hotchkiss, Benjamin Berkley 1869–1885. Born 1826. Inventor of the Hotchkiss breech-loading magazine action. Many of his patents (April 17, 1869) were bought by the United States Government. Established a plant at New Haven, Connecticut, 1869 to 1882, when the company name became **Hotchkiss & Co.** At this time, also, established an office at 113 Chambers Street, New York, New York. B. B. Hotchkiss died in 1885.

Houghton, Richard about 1850. General gunsmith at Norway, Maine.

Houston, James about 1780. Shop located at Philadelphia, Pennsylvania. General gunsmith.

Howard, S. 1862–1869. Took out his first patent October 28, 1862, at New Haven, Connecticut. The patents covered a hammerless breech-loading action applied to rifles, shotguns, and pistols. **Whitney Arms Co.** at Whitneyville, Connecticut, made most of the arms under contract.

Howe, H. about 1870. General gunsmith at Lansing, New York.

Howell, C. W. 1855–1866. Made percussion halfstock hunting rifles at Martins Ferry, Ohio.

Howell, T. about 1800. Flintlock pistol maker at Philadelphia, Pennsylvania.

Howland, Rufus J. 1840–1870. Shop located at Binghamton, New York. Made heavy caliber match percussion rifles. During Civil War had United States Government contract for percussion sharpshooters' rifles.

Hubbard, Joseph about 1850. General gunsmith at Hudson Street, Hartford, Connecticut.

Huber, Abram about 1800. Made flintlock Kentucky rifles at Manchester Township, York County, Pennsylvania.

Huber, J. about 1840. Shop located at 49 Locust Street, St. Louis, Missouri. General gunsmith.

Hudson, William L. 1852–1864. Percussion target and hunting rifle maker at Cincinnati, Ohio.

Huey, Abraham about 1850. Shop located in Tunkhannock County, Pennsylvania. Made percussion Kentucky rifles.

Hughes & Phillips 1860–1863. Plant located at Newark, New Jersey. Had United States Government contract for altering flintlock to percussion arms.

Hughes, Michael about 1800. General gunsmith at 67 Water Street, New York, New York.

Hughsted, A. 1848–1854. Shop located at Ripley, Brown County, Ohio. General gunsmith.

Hulett, Phineas 1840–1865. General gunsmith at Shaftsbury, Vermont.

Hull, Benjamin about 1835. Shop located on Sansom Street, Philadelphia, Pennsylvania. General gunsmith.

Humberger, Peter, Sr. 1774–1811. Founder of a family of Kentucky rifle makers. He was active in Lancaster County, Pennsylvania, from 1774 to 1791, when he migrated to Perry County, Ohio, and set up a shop from 1791 until his death in 1811. His son, Peter, Jr., born December 1, 1775, learned his trade under his father and set up a shop at Hopewell, Perry County, Ohio, and was active until his death April 19, 1852. Another son, Henry, had a shop in Whitely County, Indiana. Peter, Jr., had two sons. Peter III, born October 8, 1826, set up a shop at Glenford, Ohio, from 1846 and was active until his death February 11, 1899. The other son, Adam, born December 21, 1806, set up a shop at Somerset, Ohio, in 1833 and was active until his death in May, 1865.

Humble, Michael 1775–1795. Flintlock Kentucky rifle maker. Shop located at Louisville, Kentucky. It is recorded that he made a flintlock rifle to Daniel Boone's order in 1782.

Humes, Joseph about 1800. General gunsmith on Poplar Street, Philadelphia, Pennsylvania.

Hummell, F. about 1855. Percussion Kentucky rifle maker at Lebanon, Pennsylvania.

Humphreys, H. about 1800. Made Model 1795 flintlock muskets under United States Government contract at Pawtucket, Rhode Island.

Hunsicker, Henry about 1820. Flintlock Kentucky rifle maker in Lehigh County, Pennsylvania.

Hunt, David 1858–1860. General gunsmith at Cincinnati, Ohio.

Hunt, John about 1815. Shop located at North Square, Boston, Massachusetts. General gunsmith.

Hunt, Walter 1849–1853. Patented on August 21, 1849, a lever-action repeating rifle at New York, New York. This was known as the "Volition Repeater" and was the forerunner of the Henry and Winchester actions. It was.

not successful because suitable cartridges had not been perfected.

Hunter Arms Co. 1888 to date. Plant located at Fulton, New York. Made cartridge shotguns. Purchased the L. C. Smith Co. in 1888.

Hunter, David about 1775. Made flintlock muskets for the Virginia Militia in Berkeley County, Virginia.

Hunter, James 1760–1775. Flintlock musket and fowling piece maker at Falmouth, Virginia Colony. Also known as the **Rappahannock Forge.**

Huntington, Gurdon about 1800. Made Model 1795 flintlock muskets under United States Government contract at Walpole, New Hampshire.

Huntington, Hezekiah, 1775–1778. Made flintlock muskets for the Connecticut Militia at Windham, Connecticut.

Huntington, V. about 1800. Flintlock Kentucky rifle maker at Allentown, Pennsylvania.

Hurd, Jacob 1816–1825. General gunsmith at Adams Street, Boston, Massachusetts.

Huse, R. P. 1850–1870. Percussion pistol maker at Manchester, New Hampshire.

Huslace, H. G. about 1840. General gunsmith at Franklin Street, St. Louis, Missouri.

Hutchinson, Anthony about 1840. General gunsmith at 9 Chestnut Street, Rochester, New York.

Hutchinson, E. about 1850. Shop located in Baltimore, Maryland. General gunsmith.

Hutchinson, R. J. about 1830. Flintlock and, later, percussion Kentucky rifle maker at Williamsport, Pennsylvania.

Hutz, Benjamin about 1800. Shop located at Lancaster, Pennsylvania. Made flintlock Kentucky rifles.

Hyde & Shattuck 1875–1880. Plant located at Hatfield, Massachusetts. Made cartridge shotguns. In 1880 became **C. S. Shattuck & Co.**

Hyslop, R. about 1850. General gunsmith in New York, New York.

NOTES

Imhoff, Benedict about 1785. Flintlock Kentucky rifle maker in Heidelberg Township, Berks County, Pennsylvania.

Ingalls, Barney about 1840. Shop located at Morganstown, Virginia (now West Virginia). General gunsmith.

Ingalls, Brown about 1845. General gunsmith at Bangor, Maine.

Ingles, David about 1845. General gunsmith at Carondelet Street, St. Louis, Missouri.

Ingles, Samuel about 1835. Shop located at Georgetown, South Carolina. General gunsmith.

Irving, William 1861–1870. Maker of percussion revolvers and the Reed Patent (April 28, 1863) metallic cartridge revolvers at 20 Cliff Street, New York, New York.

Isaac, George about 1830. General gunsmith at Main Street, Buffalo, New York.

Isch, Christian 1774–1782. Made flintlock muskets for the Pennsylvania Militia at West King and Prince streets, Lancaster, Pennsylvania.

Ithaca Gun Co. 1880 to date. Plant at Ithaca, New York. Make cartridge shotguns.

Iver Johnson Arms Works 1871 to date. Plant located at 244 Main Street, Worcester, Massachusetts, 1871 to 1881, and at Fitchburg, Massachusetts, 1881 to date. Make metallic cartridge revolvers, shotguns, and rifles.

Ives, Joseph G. about 1850. Percussion pistol maker at 205 State Street, New Haven, Connecticut.

NOTES

Jackel, Christian about 1850. General gunsmith at Buffalo, New York.

Jackson, E. T. about 1835. Shop located at 19 Oak Street, St. Louis, Missouri. General gunsmith.

Jackson, S. about 1860. Made heavy caliber percussion rifles at Palmyra, New York.

Jacobs, B. 1866–1876. General gunsmith at Selina, Alabama.

Jacobs, Cornelius 1842–1866. Shop located at Friend Street, Columbus, Ohio, 1842 to 1845, moved to Alton, Ohio, 1845 to 1866.

Jakob, Joseph 1859–1869. Made cased percussion pistols and percussion rifles at Philadelphia, Pennsylvania. Some pieces were marked **Jacob.**

James & Ferris 1839–1861. Shop located at Utica, New York, 1839 to 1858, when partnership was dissolved and became **Morgan James,** 1858 to 1861. General gunsmith.

James, Robert about 1795. General gunsmith at 3 Thames Street, Baltimore, Maryland.

Jankofsky, Anthony about 1775. Shop located at King Street, Charleston, South Carolina. General gunsmith.

Jaquith, Elijah about 1835. General gunsmith at Brattleboro, Vermont.

Jarns, Lewis 1849–1854. General gunsmith at Athens, Ohio.

Jelt, Stephen about 1845. Shop located at 168 North First Street, St. Louis, Missouri. General gunsmith and dealer.

Jenison, J. about 1850. Made saw-handle percussion pistols at Southbridge, Massachusetts.

Jenks & Son, Alfred 1860–1867. Alfred Jenks and son, Barton H. Jenks,

located in Philadelphia, Pennsylvania, with plant at Bridesburg, Pennsylvania, had United States Government contract for Model 1861 percussion rifles.

Jenks, Stephen 1795–1814. Had United States Government contract for Model 1795 flintlock muskets at Pawtucket, Rhode Island, 1795 to 1798. Became **Jenks & Son** in 1798 and moved to North Providence, Rhode Island, from 1798 to 1814. Under government contract also made Model 1808 flintlock muskets.

Jenks, William 1839–1858. Inventor of the Jenks breech-loading percussion carbine patented May 25, 1838, at Columbia, South Carolina. These were made under United States Government contract by Remington at Herkimer, New York, and N. P. Ames at Chicopee Falls, Massachusetts.

Jenner, E. K. about 1855. General gunsmith and dealer at San Francisco, California.

Jennings, J. about 1820. Shop located at Elmira, New York. General gunsmith.

Jennings, James 1867–1875. Shop located at Fredericksburg, Virginia. General gunsmith.

Jennings, Lewis 1849–1853. Inventor and patentee of a lever-operated magazine rifle at New York, New York, December 20, 1849. This and the Walter Hunt patent were the basic patents for the Henry and, later, the Winchester rifles. Robbins and Lawrence of Windsor, Vermont, made the Jennings rifle.

Jennings, Richard 1847–1870. General gunsmith located at 10 Ontario Street, Cleveland, Ohio, 1847 to 1865, then moved to 1 Broadway, Cleveland, Ohio, 1865 to 1870.

Jetter, Jacob about 1860. General gunsmith at 118 Genesee Street, Buffalo, New York.

Jinney, B. 1849–1854. Percussion Kentucky rifle maker in Coshocton County, Ohio.

Johnson & Bro. (Gunder & Johannes) 1856–1870. General gunsmiths, made percussion hunting rifles. Shop located at 238 Third Street, St. Paul, Minnesota.

Johnson, Bye & Co. 1873–1875. Plant located at 50 Central Street, Worcester, Massachusetts. Made single shot metallic cartridge rifles.

Johnson, Henry about 1840. Shop located on Genesee Street, Buffalo, New York. General gunsmith.

Johnson, Ira N. 1850–1857. Had United States Government contract for Model 1842 Army percussion pistols. Shop located at Middletown, Connecticut.

Johnson, Robert 1822–1854. Shop located at Middletown, Connecticut. Had United States Government contract for Model 1836 Army flintlock pistols, also long arms Model 1817 flintlock rifles.

Johnson, Seth 1773–1777. Made flintlock muskets for the Massachusetts Militia at Old Rutland, Massachusetts.

Johnson, William about 1790. General gunsmith at Worcester, Massachusetts.

Johnston, John H. 1856–1889. Established a general gunsmithery at Waynesboro, Pennsylvania, in 1856 until 1865, when he moved to 179 Smithfield Street, Pittsburgh, Pennsylvania. With his son, James L. Johnston, was also owner of the **Great Western Gun Works** at 706 Smithfield Street,

Pittsburgh, Pennsylvania, established in 1865. John H. Johnston died in 1889. The business continued until 1895.

Johnston, Samuel about 1850. General gunsmith at 56 Wayne Avenue, Pittsburgh, Pennsylvania.

Jones, Amos 1774–1777. Made flintlock muskets for the Connecticut Militia at Colchester, Connecticut.

Jones, Charles & Robert (Brothers) 1775–1783. General gunsmiths at Lancaster, Pennsylvania.

Jones, John about 1700. Established a gunsmithery at Charleston, Carolina Colony.

Jones, John about 1845. Shop located at 52 Superior Street, Cleveland, Ohio. General gunsmith.

Jones, John 1848–1854. General gunsmith at Salineville, Ohio.

Jones, Joseph 1841–1848. Shop located at Columbus, Ohio. General gunsmith.

Jones, McElwaine & Co. 1860–1862. Plant located at Holly Springs, Mississippi. Owned by W. A. Jones and W. S. McElwaine. Had contract with Confederate States Government for percussion muskets.

Jones, Owen 1875–1878. Made metallic cartridge revolvers at Philadelphia, Pennsylvania.

Jorg, Jacob about 1815. Flintlock Kentucky rifle maker in Berks County, Pennsylvania.

Joslyn, Benjamin F. 1852–1878. Patentee of the Joslyn breech-loading percussion carbine, dated August 23, 1855, and the Joslyn percussion revolver patented May 4, 1858. Established the **Joslyn Arms Co.** at Stonington, Connecticut, in 1861. Had United

States Government contract for both the revolvers and carbines. Both arms were also made by W. C. Freeman at Worcester, and the carbines by A. H. Waters & Co. at Millbury, Massachusetts. The Joslyn Arms Co. closed in 1878.

Joslyn, Isaac M. about 1860. General gunsmith on Jackson Street, Batavia, New York.

Jost, Caspar 1775–1784. General gunsmith, made flintlock muskets for the Pennsylvania Militia in White Plains Township, Dauphin County, Pennsylvania.

Joy, Andrew about 1845. Shop located on Market Street, Pittsburgh, Pennsylvania. General gunsmith.

Jughard, Charles 1859–1869. General gunsmith at Main and North Streets, Fostoria, Ohio.

Justice, Philip S. about 1860. Had United States Government contract for Model 1863 percussion rifles. Located at Philadelphia, Pennsylvania.

NOTES

Kansteiner, William 1847–1890. General gunsmith at Hannibal, Missouri.

Kascheline, Peter about 1775. Made flintlock muskets for the Pennsylvania Militia in Northampton County, Pennsylvania.

Kearling, Samuel about 1780. Kentucky flintlock rifle maker in Bucks County, Pennsylvania.

Keeler, Lucius about 1840. General gunsmith at St. Albans, Vermont.

Keeley, Mathias & Sebastian about 1775. Made flintlock muskets for the Pennsylvania Militia at Philadelphia, Pennsylvania.

Keen, J. C. 1876–1880. General gunsmith at Joliet, Illinois.

Keen, Walker & Co. 1861–1863. E. F. Keen and James M. Walker had a contract with the Confederate States and probably made the Confederate Reed Patent carbine. Plant at Danville, Virginia.

Keener, Jacob, John & Peter (Brothers) 1796–1831. General gunsmiths at Green Street (now Exeter Street), Baltimore, Maryland.

Keener, Samuel about 1775. Probably father of Jacob, John, and Peter Keener. General gunsmith at Baltimore, Maryland.

Keffer, Jacob about 1800. Flintlock Kentucky rifle maker at Lancaster, Pennsylvania.

Kehler, John about 1805. Shop located at Lancaster, Pennsylvania. Made flintlock Kentucky rifles.

Keim, John 1821–1839. Flintlock Kentucky rifle maker at Reading, Pennsylvania.

Kelher & Bro. 1870–1873. General gunsmiths at Harrisburg, Pennsylvania.

Kellar, about 1850. Percussion Kentucky rifle maker at Maryville, Tennessee.

Keller, C. about 1860. Maker of percussion hunting rifles at Evansville, Indiana.

Keller, John 1823–1842. Flintlock and, later, percussion Kentucky rifle maker at Carlisle, Pennsylvania.

Kellog, Wells & Co. about 1835. General gunsmiths and dealers at 176 Main Street, Cincinnati, Ohio.

Kellogg, E. C. 1859–1871. General gunsmith at Hartford, Connecticut, 1859 to 1871. Name changed to **Kellogg & Co.,** 1871 to 1875.

Kellogg, Henry & Alfred A. (Brothers) 1862–1876. General gunsmiths. Henry active 1862 to 1867 at New Haven, Connecticut, and Alfred A. active at 202 State Street, New Haven, Connecticut, 1867 to 1876.

Kemmerer, David about 1850. General gunsmith at Lehighton, Carbon County, Pennsylvania.

Kempton, Ephriam about 1680. Gunsmith at Salem and later at Boston, Massachusetts Colony.

Kendall, Nicanor 1835–1850. Born December 20, 1807. Established a shop at Windsor, Vermont, in 1835. Made underhammer percussion rifles and pistols. Name changed to **Kendall & Co.** 1838 to 1842, and **Kendall & Lawrence** 1842 to 1850. Nicanor Kendall died December 24, 1861.

Kennedy, Martin F. 1864–1870. General gunsmith at 163 Third Street, St. Paul, Minnesota.

Kerlin, John, Sr. & Jr. 1775–1814. John Kerlin, Sr., made flintlock muskets for the Pennsylvania Militia in Chester County, Pennsylvania. In 1801 John Kerlin, Jr., took over the shop and later received a United States Government contract for Model 1808 flintlock muskets.

Kern, Frederick & Reinhart (Brothers) about 1855. General gunsmiths at Lancaster, Pennsylvania.

Kern, Michael about 1790. Shop located at 448 North Front Street, Philadelphia, Pennsylvania. General gunsmith.

Kessler, John 1845–1858. General gunsmith at Weston, Missouri.

Kider, John about 1835. Shop located on Washington Street, Philadelphia, Pennsylvania. General gunsmith.

Kile, Nathan about 1815. General gunsmith in Jackson County, Ohio.

Kilpatrick, David about 1860. Made heavy caliber percussion rifles at Philadelphia, Pennsylvania.

Kinder, Samuel about 1775. Maker of flintlock muskets for the Pennsylvania Militia at Philadelphia, Pennsylvania.

King, Frederick about 1855. General gunsmith at Lancaster, Pennsylvania.

King, P. P. 1845–1885. Shop located at Celina, Ohio. General gunsmith.

Kingsley, Henry about 1865. Patented a metallic cartridge pistol. Models made at Hartford, Connecticut. No production recorded.

Kinsley, Adam 1795–1812. Had United States Government contract for Model 1795 flintlock muskets and, later, contract for Model 1808 flintlock muskets. Shop located at Bridgewater, Massachusetts.

Kinter, John Simon 1820–1851. Made flintlock and, later, percussion Kentucky rifles. Shop located in Harrison County, Indiana.

Kirchberg, William about 1840. General gunsmith at Philadelphia, Pennsylvania.

Kirkman, John about 1780. Flintlock Kentucky rifle maker at Ashville, Pennsylvania.

Kirkwood, David 1882–1886. Shop located at 23 Elm Street, Boston, Massachusetts. General gunsmith.

Kirlin, John & Samuel (Brothers) about 1800. Made flintlock muskets for the Pennsylvania Militia at Philadelphia, Pennsylvania.

Kirschman, E. about 1835. General gunsmith at Danville, Pennsylvania.

Kistler, George about 1800. Flintlock Kentucky rifle maker in Berks County, Pennsylvania.

Kittinger, J. 1840–1860. Made percussion rifles at Charleston, Virginia (now West Virginia).

Kittridge, B. 1845–1891. General gunsmith and dealer at 236 Main Street, Cincinnati, Ohio, 1845 to 1851. Became Eaton & Kittridge, 134 Main Street, 1851 to 1859. Then became Kittridge & Co. at same address, 1859 to 1891. Established a branch at 55 St. Charles Street, New Orleans, Louisiana about 1870.

Klattenhoff, John about 1875. General gunshop at Colorado Springs, Colorado.

Kleinhenn, Emanuel about 1860. Shop located at Franklin Avenue, St. Louis, Missouri. General gunsmith.

Kleist, Daniel 1780–1792. Maker of flintlock Kentucky rifles at Bethlehem, Pennsylvania, 1780 to 1785, and at Easton, Pennsylvania, 1785 to 1792.

Klepzig, J. C. 1855–1858. General gunsmith and dealer at San Francisco, California.

Kliemeken, H. 1870–1875. Shop located at Trinidad, Colorado. General gunsmith.

Kline, Conrad about 1780. Flintlock Kentucky rifle and pistol maker at Lancaster, Pennsylvania.

Kline, Jacob about 1840. Shop located in Frankfort Township, Cumberland County, Pennsylvania. Made flintlock Kentucky rifles.

Klinedinst, Andrew about 1825. General gunsmith at South Beaver Street, York, Pennsylvania.

Knappenberger, Henry about 1820. Flintlock Kentucky rifle maker in Malford Township, Lehigh County, Pennsylvania.

Knowlton, W. 1849–1854. General gunsmith at Lee, Athens County, Ohio.

Koch, John N. 1851–1899. Born in Switzerland in 1829, emigrated to the United States in 1851 and set up a gunshop at Rock Island, Illinois. Made percussion match and target rifles. Active until 1899.

Kochler, P. about 1850. Made percussion Kentucky rifles at Lewisburg, Pennsylvania.

Koehler, Hans Frederick 1860–1880. Born in Germany in 1833, emigrated to the United States in 1860. Established a general gunsmithery at Newport, Kentucky. Active until his death in 1880.

Kohl, Conrad 1851–1862. General gunsmithery at Reading, Pennsylvania.

Kraft, Jacob 1771–1782. Flintlock Kentucky rifle maker at Lancaster, Pennsylvania.

Kraft, P. W. about 1840. Made cased percussion dueling pistols at Columbia, South Carolina.

Krammer, Henry about 1860. General gunsmith at 163 Bowery, Albany, New York.

Kretzel, A. about 1855. Made percussion rifles and pistols at Jerseyville, Illinois.

Kreutner, C. 1869–1875. Shop located at Montgomery, Alabama. Made percussion rifles.

Krider, John 1839–1870. Shop located at Second and Walnut Streets, Philadelphia, Pennsylvania. General gunsmith and dealer. Made long arms and percussion derringer-type pistols.

Krueger, H. 1875–1880. General gunsmith at 10 Second Street, Minneapolis, Minnesota.

Krueger, J. W. about 1865. Shop located at Walker Valley, New York. General gunsmith.

Kryter, Charles 1870–1876. General gunsmith at 115 Market Street, Wheeling, West Virginia.

Kuhns, Peter about 1820. Flintlock Kentucky rifle maker in Whitehall Township, Lehigh County, Pennsylvania.

Kunkle, 1810–1814. General gunsmith at Philadelphia, Pennsylvania.

Kuntz, Michael about 1800. Shop located at Lancaster, Pennsylvania. Made flintlock Kentucky rifles.

Kunz, Jacob 1770–1817. Made flintlock brass barrel pistols. Shop located on Germantown Road, Philadelphia, Pennsylvania.

Kussmaul, William J. about 1860. General gunsmith at Baltimore, Maryland.

NOTES

Labeau, J. B. 1835–1848. General gunsmith at 120 First Street, St. Louis, Missouri.

Lacave, C. about 1880. Shop located at Canton, Ohio. General gunsmith.

Ladd, Wilson about 1850. General gunsmith at Dorset, Vermont.

Laget, J. about 1850. General gunsmith at New Orleans, Louisiana.

Laib, Charles about 1860. Shop located at Madison, Wisconsin. General gunsmith.

Lakenan, James about 1830. General gunsmith at Main Street, St. Louis, Missouri.

Lamb, Anderson 1865–1875. Made percussion rifles at Jamestown, Guilford County, North Carolina.

Lamb & Co., H. C. 1861–1865. Plant at Jamestown, near Greensboro, North Carolina. Had Confederate States contract for percussion rifles. This plant was destroyed when Federal troops occupied North Carolina in 1865.

Lambert, Roger about 1835. Made percussion rifles at Lyme, New Hampshire.

Lamson & Co., E. G. 1851–1867. Plant located at Windsor, Vermont. In 1861, the name changed to **Lamson, Goodnow & Yale** (E. G. Lamson, A. F. Goodnow and B. B. Yale) and also established an additional plant at Shellburn Falls, Massachusetts. Had United States Government contract for Model 1861 Springfield percussion rifles, these marked on lockplate "L.G. & Y." Also, a government contract for Ball and Lamson percussion carbines. Business closed in 1867.

Lamson, Truman about 1840. General gunsmith at Bennington, Vermont.

Lane & Read 1826–1836. Made Model 1816 flintlock muskets at Boston, Massachusetts, for the Massachusetts Militia.

Langdon, W. C. 1857–1866. Made heavy target percussion rifles and sharpshooter percussion rifles during Civil War. Shop located at Boston, Massachusetts.

Larosh, Jesse about 1820. Flintlock Kentucky rifle maker in Lehigh County, Pennsylvania.

Larson, W. about 1830. Shop located at Harrisburg, Pennsylvania. General gunsmith.

Lash, J. about 1815. General gunsmith at Marrsville, Ohio.

Latham, Richard about 1770. General gunsmith and dealer on King Street, Charleston, South Carolina.

Latil, L. A. about 1855. Percussion pistol maker and general gunsmith at Baton Rouge, Louisiana.

Lawrence, Richard S. 1838–1855. Shop located at Windsor, Vermont. In 1843 formed a partnership with Nicanor Kendall and S. E. Robbins under the name of **Robins, Kendall & Lawrence.** Made percussion rifles and shotguns. The firm failed in 1855.

Lawrence, Thomas about 1850. Percussion rifle maker and general gunsmith at Lancaster, Pennsylvania.

Lawrence, William 1857–1868. Maker of percussion pistols and rifles at Milford, Massachusetts.

Lawser, William H. 1852–1876. General gunsmith at 430 Market Street, Harrisburg, Pennsylvania.

Lawton, Thomas 1831–1836. Shop located at Baltimore, Maryland. General gunsmith.

Laydendecker, George 1774–1783. Flintlock Kentucky rifle maker at Allentown, Pennsylvania.

Layland, William about 1845. Made percussion pistols and longarms at 82 Oliver Street, New York, New York.

Leader, Richard about 1650. Established a gunsmithery at Boston, Massachusetts Bay Colony.

Leamans, about 1740. Gunsmithery at Charlottesville, North Carolina.

Leaming, F. about 1800. Made flintlock Kentucky rifles at Philadelphia, Pennsylvania.

Leatherman, Fred 1862–1879. General gunsmith at Dayton, Ohio.

Leavitt, Daniel 1837–1841. Patentee of a percussion revolver on April 29, 1837, at Hartford, Connecticut.

Lechler, Henry 1848–1857. Made percussion Kentucky rifles at Lancaster, Pennsylvania.

Ledler, J. A. about 1850. Shop located at Philadelphia, Pennsylvania. Made percussion rifles and pistols.

Lee Arms Co. about 1875. Plant located at Wilkes-Barre, Pennsylvania. Made metallic cartridge revolvers.

Lee Firearms Co. 1864–1885. James Paris Lee invented the Lee metallic cartridge carbine, patented July 22, 1862, and received a United States Government contract for the manufacture of these arms. Plant located at Milwaukee, Wisconsin. On November 4, 1879, he received patents for the Lee magazine rifle and formed the **Lee Arms Co.** at Bridgeport, Connecticut. However, these rifles were made under contract by the Remington Arms Co. at Ilion, New York.

Lee, William about 1845. General gunsmith and dealer at 456 Hudson Street, New York, New York.

Leech & Rigdon 1862–1865. Thomas S. Leech and Charles H. Rigdon had a Confederate States contract for percussion revolvers patterned after Colt models. Due to the movement of the battle fronts, the plant was moved a number of times. Located at Memphis, Tennessee, in 1862, moved to Columbus, Mississippi, 1862 and 1863, to Greensboro, Georgia, in 1863. In January 1864, the company was dissolved, and Charles H. Rigdon formed a new company to take over the contracts. With Jesse A. Ansley, formed **Rigdon & Ansley & Co.**, plant on Marbury Street, Augusta, Georgia, and continued until 1865, when destroyed by Federal forces.

Leete, William about 1850. General gunsmith and dealer at 96 Perry Street, New York, New York.

Lefever, D. M. 1861–1892. Made percussion target and match rifles at Main Street, Canandaigua, New York, and, later, metallic cartridge rifles at 78 East Water Street, Syracuse, New York. In 1892, the name was changed to **Lefever Arms Co.** and located at 107 North Franklin Street, Syracuse, New York, 1892 to 1906. Purchased by the **Ithaca Gun Company** in 1918.

Lefever, Philip 1731–1766. Born in 1710 at Esopus, New York. Migrated to Pennsylvania in 1731 and set up a gunsmithery at Beaver Valley, Lancaster County, Pennsylvania. Made flintlock Kentucky rifles and did general gunsmithing.

Lefever, Samuel about 1770. Flintlock Kentucky rifle maker at Lancaster County, Pennsylvania.

Lehman, G. F. 1848–1854. General gunsmith at Jerome, Union County, Ohio.

Leitner, Adam, Ignatius, Jacob (Brothers) 1779–1810. Flintlock Kentucky rifle makers at York, Pennsylvania. Also, had United States Government contract for holster flintlock pistols.

Leland, M. L. about 1845. General gunsmith at Augusta, Maine.

Leman, Heinreich 1730–1750. Founder of the famous family of Pennsylvania gunsmiths and Kentucky rifle makers. Established a gunsmithery at Lancaster, Pennsylvania, in 1730 and was active until 1750. His son, Peter, active 1745 to 1796. Peter's son, Henry E., active 1796 to 1835, and son, Henry E., Jr., had a shop at Walnut and Cherry Streets, Lancaster, Pennsylvania, 1834 to 1860 and on East James Street, 1860 to 1867. His first United States Government contract was dated November 7, 1837, for percussion rifles and he also took over United States Government contract converting flintlock muskets to percussion. During the Civil War, Henry E., Jr., also made special sharpshooters rifles. Some of these government contract rifles were marked "CONESTOGA RIFLE WORKS, Lancaster, Pennsylvania."

LeMat, Jean Alexander Francois 1856–1865. Dr. LeMat was a Creole physician in New Orleans, Louisiana. On October 21, 1856, he received a United States Government patent for a single-action percussion revolver with a cylinder of 9 shots .42 caliber. It had under the revolver barrel a smoothbore barrel of .60 caliber which could be loaded with either ball or buckshot. The hammer had a moveable head which struck either the cap cones on the cylinder or the cone for the single barrel. With the outbreak of the Civil War, Dr. LeMat was commissioned a colonel in the Confederate Army and turned his patent over to the Confederate States. He was awarded a contract for 5000 Army percussion revolvers as described and 2000 Navy percussion revolvers (cylinder 9 shot .35 caliber, and shot barrel .50 caliber) by the Confederate Government. He went to Paris and established a partnership with Girard & Son for the manufacture of the revolvers. These were fabricated in France, and the Navy models were shipped to England for inspection and proving. A LeMat revolving carbine was also made in limited numbers. This was 38 inches over-all with 20½-inch part octagonal barrel. Cylinder was interchangeable with the Army model revolver.

Lennard, about 1770. Shop located at Lancaster, Pennsylvania. General gunsmith.

Lennox, Andrew about 1835. General gunsmith at Fairview near Pittsburgh, Pennsylvania.

Lenz, Michael about 1805. Shop located at 36 Laight Street, Baltimore, Maryland. General gunsmith.

Leonard, Artemus 1843–1849. Shop located at Saxtons River, Vermont, 1843 to 1849. Name changed to A. Leonard & Sons, 1849 to 1860, same location. Made hunting and match or target rifles.

Leonard, C. 1865–1875. General gunsmith at Petersburg, Virginia.

Leonard, Eliphalet 1775–1780. Flintlock musket maker for the Massachusetts Militia. Shop located at Easton, Massachusetts. His son, Jonathan, established a gunshop in 1778 at Stoughton, Massachusetts, which later became Canton, Massachusetts, and Jonathan's son, Charles, came in the business early in 1800. They received a United States Government contract for Model 1808 flintlock muskets, and Charles Leonard was active until 1826.

Leonard, George 1850–1855. Made percussion pepperboxes at Charlestown, Massachusetts. Patent dated

September 18, 1849. Feature was saw-handle grip.

Leonard, George O. 1859–1869. General gunsmith at Keene, New Hampshire.

Lepper, Lewis 1849–1857. General gunsmith at Lancaster, Pennsylvania.

Lester, L. M. & G. H. 1875–1885. General gunsmiths and dealers at 252 Broadway, New York, New York. Made metallic cartridge revolvers with a safety lock patent.

Lether, Jacob 1777–1820. Born December 29, 1755. Established gunshop at York, Pennsylvania, in 1777. Made flintlock Kentucky rifles and had United States Government contract for Model 1795 and later Model 1808 flintlock muskets. Active until 1820, died April 20, 1835.

Lewis, Charles about 1835. General gunsmithery on Perry Street, Buffalo, New York.

Lewis, Colonel Fielding 1752–1781. General gunsmith at Fredericksburg, Virginia. Made flintlock muskets for the Virginia Militia. Brother-in-law of General George Washington, married Washington's sister, Elizabeth.

Lewis, Joseph about 1840. General gunsmith at 13 Pell Street, New York, New York.

Lewis, Morgan about 1880. Shop located at 22 Market Street, Youngstown, Ohio. General gunsmith.

Lewis, Nelson 1810–1852. General gunsmith at 84 Congress Street, Troy, New York. Made flintlock dueling pistols and was noted for fine workmanship. Later made percussion match or target rifles. His son, James, carried on the business after his death in 1852 until 1861.

Libeau, V. G. W. 1835–1847. Made percussion revolvers at New Orleans, Louisiana, · all handmade similar to early Colt models.

Liddle, Robert 1857–1872. General gunsmith and dealer at 418 Washington Street, San Francisco, California. Name changed to **Liddle & Kaeding,** 1872 to 1889, and **Liddle Gun Co.,** 1889 to 1894.

Light, Peter about 1775. Flintlock musket maker for the Virginia Militia. Shop located in Berkeley County, Virginia.

Lightner, Ignatius about 1785. Flintlock Kentucky rifle maker in York County, Pennsylvania.

Lindner, Edward 1856–1865. Patented a percussion breech-loading carbine dated March 29, 1859. Had United States Government contract and plant in New York, New York.

Lindsay, John Parker 1860–1869. Patented a two-shot percussion rifle, dated October 9, 1860, at New York, New York. The method of firing was two charges in a single barrel, two hammers and a single trigger. Lindsay received a United States Government contract on December 17, 1863, and established the **J. P. Lindsay Manufacturing Co.** at 208 Orange Street, New Haven, Connecticut, 1864 to 1867 and at 20 Howard Street, New Haven, Connecticut, 1867 to 1869, for the fabrication of the arms.

Lins, Adam Frederick 1851–1875. Shop located in Philadelphia, Pennsylvania. Made derringer-type percussion pistols and some cased pairs.

Lipphardt, Charles 1849–1854. General gunsmith at New Richmond, Ohio.

Little, Charles about 1830. Shop located on Main Street, Providence, Rhode Island. General gunsmith.

Little, James about 1850. General gunsmith at 4 Carson Street, Pittsburgh, Pennsylvania.

Livingston, John 1795–1801. Shop located at Walpole, New Hampshire. Had United States Government contract for Model 1795 flintlock muskets.

Livingston, J. W. about 1855. General gunsmith at Syracuse, New York. Made target percussion rifles of excellent workmanship.

Llwelyn, Matthew about 1740. Established a gunsmithery at Lancaster, Pennsylvania Colony.

Loder, about 1770. Flintlock Kentucky rifle maker at Lancaster, Pennsylvania.

Loesch, Jacob about 1785. General gunsmith at Salem, North Carolina.

Lombard & Co., R. C. 1859–1870. Plant located on Market Street, Springfield, Massachusetts. Made metallic cartridge single-shot pistols.

Long, James 1865–1886. General gunsmith, made percussion rifles. Shop at Yeagerstown, Pennsylvania.

Long, Joseph about 1825. Flintlock Kentucky rifle maker in Snyder County, Pennsylvania.

Longstreth & Cook about 1770. General gunsmiths, made flintlock Kentucky rifles at Philadelphia, Pennsylvania.

Loomis, Earl about 1850. Made percussion hunting rifles at Hamilton, New York.

Loos, F. about 1860. Shop located at Albany, New York, made target percussion rifles.

Lorney, M. about 1810. Made flintlock Kentucky rifles at Boalsburg, Pennsylvania.

Losey, B. about 1850. Maker of percussion rifles at Syracuse, New York.

Lotz, Peter about 1855. Percussion Kentucky rifle maker at Lancaster, Pennsylvania.

Lovell, J. P. 1840–1870. General gunsmith and dealer at 27 Dock Street, Philadelphia, became J. P. Lovell & Sons at 147 Washington Street, Philadelphia, Pennsylvania, 1870 to 1891.

Low, William 1811–1818. Shop located in Seneca County, New York. General gunsmith, made flintlock muskets for the New York Militia.

Lowe, William V. about 1875. General gunsmith at Woburn, Massachusetts.

Lowell Arms Co. 1864–1880. Plant located on Willey Street, Lowell, Massachusetts. Made percussion and metallic cartridge revolvers.

Lower, John P. 1850–1876. General gunsmith in Philadelphia, Pennsylvania, 1850 to 1872, then moved to 281 Blake Street, Denver, Colorado in 1872. Active until 1876.

Lowery, David 1774–1777. Shop located at Weatherfield, Connecticut. General gunsmith.

Lowndes, Edward about 1870. General gunsmith at Greeley, Colorado.

Ludington, 1760–1775. Shop located at Lancaster, Pennsylvania. General gunsmithery.

Lull, Charles about 1835. General gunsmith at 33 North State Street, Rochester, New York.

Lunsmann, Francis about 1845. Shop located at 105 Second Street, St. Louis, Missouri. General gunsmith.

Lupus, A. about 1860. Made percussion underhammer pistols at Dover, New Hampshire.

Lurch, David & Joseph (Brothers) 1869–1875. General gunsmiths and dealers at Grand Street, New York, New York. Made percussion sporting and match rifles.

Lydick, Peter 1773–1779. Made flintlock muskets for the Maryland Militia. Shop located in Baltimore, Maryland.

Lyon, Warren about 1825. General gunsmith at 284 Main Street, Providence, Rhode Island.

NOTES

MacFarlane, Andrew about 1845. Maker of percussion pistols and rifles at 5 Dey Street, New York, New York.

Macon Armory 1862–1865. Confederate States Armory at Macon, Georgia. Made percussion pistols. Destroyed by General Winslow's Federal troops, April 17, 1865.

Maltby, Henly & Co. 1878–1890. Plant located at New York, New York. Made metallic cartridge revolvers under the John T. Smith patents (March 11, 1884). These revolvers were issued to the Metropolitan Police Force, New York, New York.

Manhattan Firearms Mfg. Co. 1840–1870. Plant located at Newark, New Jersey, 1840 to 1860. Made percussion pistols and pepperboxes. In 1864, opened offices in New York, New York, and established a plant at Brooklyn, New York. Made percussion revolvers similar to Colt Navy models and were forced to close the business in 1870 by Colt lawsuit for infringement of patents.

Mann, M. D. about 1820. General gunsmith on Main Street, Buffalo, New York.

Manning, Richard about 1750. Gunsmith at Ipswich, Massachusetts.

Mapother, Dillon H. about 1870. Shop located at Louisville, Kentucky. General gunsmith.

Marble, Simeon about 1850. General gunsmith at Sunderland, Vermont.

Marcum, J. E. about 1850. Made percussion target and match rifles at New York, New York.

Marker, Paul 1867–1875. General gunsmith at Union City, Indiana.

Marlin, John Mahlon 1870–1880. Made C. H. Ballard patent (April 9, 1867) rifles and metallic cartridge derringers at New Haven, Connecticut. The following are the succeeding names of the companies: **Marlin Firearms Co.** 1880 to 1915, **Marlin Arms Corp.** 1915 to 1916, **Marlin Rockwell Corp.** 1916 to 1921, **Marlin Firearms Co.** 1921 to date, all at New Haven, Connecticut.

Marsh, J. 1850–1870. Shop located at Binghamton, New York. General gunsmith.

Marsh, Johnson about 1835. General gunsmith at Dorset, Vermont.

Marsten, E. about 1850. General gunsmith at Concord, New Hampshire.

Marsters, William about 1845. General gunsmith at Twentieth Street and Broadway, New York, New York.

Marston, David about 1835. Shop located at 179 North Fourth Street, Philadelphia, Pennsylvania. General gunsmith.

Marston, S. about 1845. Made percussion pistols and rifles at 197 Allen Street, New York, New York.

Marston, William W. 1850–1863. Plant located at Second Avenue and Twenty-second Street, New York, New York. Patentee and maker of the sliding breech lock (June 18, 1850), also made percussion pepperboxes, pistols and revolvers. Later made three-shot, three-barrel metallic cartridge pistol of derringer type. Plant also known as the **Phoenix Armory.** Firm name was changed to **Marston & Knox** in 1862. The armory was burned during the Draft Riots in New York on July 13, 1863.

Martin, Charles about 1850. General gunsmith at 74 Market Street, Hartford, Connecticut.

Martin, George H. about 1850. Shop located at 39 Portland Street, Worcester, Massachusetts. General gunsmith.

Martin, Robert about 1810. General gunsmith at 20 Frederick Street, Baltimore, Maryland.

Martin & Smith about 1845. Made percussion rifles and pistols at 98 Market Street, Philadelphia, Pennsylvania.

Maslin, M. about 1800. Made flintlock Kentucky rifles at Lancaster, Pennsylvania.

Mason, J. C. about 1840. General gunsmith at Keene, New Hampshire.

Mason, William 1862–1874. Plant located at Taunton, Massachusetts. Had United States Government contract for Model 1861 percussion rifles.

Massa, George about 1855. General gunsmith and percussion Kentucky rifle maker at Lancaster, Pennsylvania.

Massachusetts Arms Co. 1850– 1866. Founded by Daniel B. Wesson at Chicopee Falls, Massachusetts, to manufacture percussion revolvers based on the Edwin Wesson patents. Daniel B. Wesson inherited these patents on the death of Edwin Wesson, his older brother. In August 1859, Colonel Colt forced the discontinuance of manufacture by an infringement of patent lawsuit. The company had several United States Government contracts during the Civil War, making Green, Maynard and Smith percussion carbines and Adams (British patent) percussion revolvers. Daniel B. Wesson was also one of the partners of Smith & Wesson at Norwich, Connecticut.

Massey, Benjamin about 1730. Gunsmithery at Tradd Street, Charleston, South Carolina.

Massey, Philip about 1735. General gunsmith on King Street, Charleston, South Carolina.

Matheson, Welcome about 1770. Made flintlock muskets for Rhode Island Militia, location in Rhode Island not known.

Matson, Thomas & John 1655–1682. Gunsmithery at Boston, Massachusetts Bay Colony.

Maurer, John about 1800. Flintlock Kentucky rifle maker at Lancaster, Pennsylvania.

Maxwell & Co., A. L. 1860–1863. Made Model 1841 percussion muskets for the State of Tennessee at Knoxville, Tennessee, during the Civil War. The plant was destroyed by Federal troops November 23, 1863.

Mayer, George 1819–1838. Made flintlock Kentucky rifles at Lancaster, Pennsylvania.

Mayesch 1770–1775. Flintlock musket maker and general gunsmith at Lancaster, Pennsylvania.

Maynard Arms Co. 1851–1865. Dr. Edward Maynard, a dental surgeon in Washington, District of Columbia, invented and patented the Maynard Primer (September 22, 1845) and later patented the Maynard percussion breech-loading system (May 27, 1851). The Maynard Primer was a roll tape of percussion caps, a cap moving over the nipple of a percussion arm at each cocking of the hammer. The Primer was submitted to a Board of Ordnance at West Point, New York, in 1845 and approved by the Board for United States arms. The Primer was improved in 1851 as part of the lock plate and became the Model of 1855 on pistols, rifles and muskets. The Maynard percussion breech-loading carbines were made under United States Government contract with the **Maynard Arms**

Co. at the plant of the Massachusetts Arms Co. at Chickopee Falls, Massachusetts.

McAllister, B. 1859–1868. General gunsmith at Lawrence, Massachusetts.

McAllister, C. about 1855. Shop located at 343 King Street, Charleston, South Carolina. General gunsmith.

McCain, Hugh about 1800. General gunsmith in Allegheny County, Pennsylvania.

McCartney, Robert 1805–1818. General gunsmith at Boston, Massachusetts.

McCartney, William G. about 1850. Percussion Kentucky rifle maker at 300 Liberty Street, Pittsburgh, Pennsylvania.

McClellan, Hugh about 1820. General gunsmith at 16 Beaver Street, Albany, New York.

McClure, J. M. 1848–1854. Shop located at Bucyrus, Ohio. General gunsmith.

McComas, Alexander 1843–1875. General gunsmith at 51 Calvert Street, Baltimore, Maryland.

McComas, Nicholas 1853–1869. Shop located at 44 Pratt Street, Baltimore, Maryland. Dealer and general gunsmith.

McCormick, Robert 1796–1802. An Irish immigrant, established a gunshop at Globe Mill, Germantown Road, Philadelphia, Pennsylvania. Had United States Government contract for Model 1795 flintlock muskets and dragoon flintlock pistols.

McCosh, Samuel about 1840. General gunsmith and maker of percussion Kentucky rifles at 22 Diamond Street, Pittsburgh, Pennsylvania.

McCoy, Alexander about 1780. Shop located on Dock Street, Philadelphia, Pennsylvania. General gunsmith.

McCoy, Kester about 1770. Flintlock Kentucky rifle maker in Paxton Township, Lancaster County, Pennsylvania.

McCullough, George 1771–1775. General gunsmith in Lancaster County, Pennsylvania.

McGillvery, 1854–1860. Shop located at Symmes Corner, Butler County, Ohio. General gunsmith.

McGirr, A. C. 1856–1885. General gunsmith and percussion rifle maker at Marietta, Ohio.

McGovern, Anthony 1858–1876. Shop located at Madison, Wisconsin. General gunsmith.

McHarg, J. B. about 1860. General gunsmith at 35 James Street, Rome, New York.

McKenny & Bean 1866–1871. General gunsmiths at 166 Main Street, Biddleford, Maine.

McKim Bros. 1800–1845. Made flintlock and, later, percussion pistols at Baltimore, Maryland.

McLarty, William about 1845. General gunsmith and dealer at 109 Cherry Street, New York, New York.

McMahon, John about 1845. Shop located at 87 Oliver Street, New York, New York. General gunsmith.

McMant, John about 1835. General gunsmith at Wellsburg, Virginia (now West Virginia). Made flintlock Kentucky rifles.

McNaught about 1810. Shop located at Richmond, Virginia. General gunsmith.

McNearney, Michael about 1855. General gunsmith and dealer at 114 Church Street, Charleston, South Carolina.

McRae, Alexander 1815–1821. Shop located at Richmond, Virginia. Had United States Government contract for Model 1812 flintlock muskets.

Meakin, Benjamin 1855–1870. General gunsmith at New Paltz, New York.

Meakin, George about 1845. Shop located at 58 Chatham Street, New York, New York. Made percussion pistols and rifles.

Mears, John about 1795. General gunsmith at 2 Beresford Street, Charleston, South Carolina.

Medbury, Joseph 1826–1838. Shop located at 31 Buffalo Street, Rochester, New York.

Medbury, Thomas & Isaac (Son) 1800–1828. Made flintlock rifles and fowling pieces at Erieville, New York.

Meier, Adolphus 1845–1860. Maker of percussion pistols and rifles at St. Louis, Missouri.

Meissener, Charles 1856–1880. General gunsmith at 12 South Sixth Street, Zanesville, Ohio. Became Meissener & Son 1880 to 1902 at same address.

Melchoir, Nathaniel 1830–1840. Shop located on Mercer Street, Baltimore, Maryland. Made percussion rifles of fine workmanship.

Mendenhall, Jones & Gardner 1862–1865. Cyrus P. Mendenhall, Ezekiel P. Jones and Grafton Gardner established a rifle plant at Jamestown near Greensboro, North Carolina. Had a Confederate States contract for Model 1841 percussion rifles. These rifles were marked "M. J. & G. N. C. C. S."

(Mendenhall, Jones & Gardner— North Carolina—Confederate States.). Federal cavalry destroyed the plant in April 1865.

Merckley, Jacob about 1785. General gunsmith at Philadelphia, Pennsylvania.

Meredith, Benjamin about 1815. Shop located on Paca Street, Baltimore, Maryland. General gunsmith.

Meriden Arms Co. 1863–1890. Plant located at Meriden, Connecticut. Had United States Government contracts during Civil War and later various State Militia contracts. Made Miller patent (May 23, 1865) breech-loading rifle and Spencer carbine (February 4, 1862), also Triplett and Scott repeating breech-loading carbines and rifles (patent December 6, 1864). Later metallic cartridge revolvers of the Fryburg patent.

Merrill Patent Firearms Mfg. Co. 1852–1869. James H. Merrill inventor, patentee (January 8, 1856) and maker of the Merrill percussion breech-loading system operated by a lever-type breechblock. Plant located at Baltimore, Maryland. Had United States Government contract during Civil War for percussion breech-loading carbines and rifles.

Merrimac Arms & Mfg. Co. 1866–1869. Plant located at Newburyport, Massachusetts. Had United States Government contract for C. H. Ballard patent (November 5, 1861 and April 9, 1867) breech-loading carbines and rifles.

Merriman, Silas about 1775. Made flintlock muskets for the Connecticut Militia. Shop location in Connecticut not known.

Merritt, Alan about 1855. General gunsmith at East Randolph, Massachusetts.

Merritt, Ira 1859–1868. General gunsmith at Abington, Massachusetts.

Merritt, John 1789–1798. Shop located at Adams Street, Boston, Massachusetts. General gunsmith.

Mershon, Ralph S. 1855–1863. Shop located at Zanesville, Ohio. General gunsmith.

Merwin & Bray 1853–1864. Located at 245 Broadway, New York, New York. Were dealers and sales agents for various types of firearms with their name on the arms. The firm name was changed to **Merwin, Taylor & Simpkins** at same address 1864 to 1868, and they, also, had a plant at Worcester, Massachusetts, during this period. In 1868, the name was changed to **Merwin, Hulbert & Co.** and moved to 83 Chambers Street, New York, and under this name patented (January 24, 1874) an Army model 1876 metallic cartridge revolver. These were made under United States Government contract at the plant of Hopkins and Allen, Norwich, Connecticut. These revolvers were also sold to foreign governments by Merwin, Hulbert & Co. They were still located at 83 Chambers Street until 1887, when they moved to 26 West 23rd Street, New York, New York. The business was closed in 1891.

Messersmith, John & Jacob 1779–1802. Flintlock Kentucky rifle makers at Lancaster, Pennsylvania.

Messersmith, Samuel 1775–1778. Made flintlock muskets for the Maryland Militia. Shop located at Baltimore, Maryland.

Metropolitan Arms Co. 1859–1867. Arms dealers and manufacturers at 97 Pearl Street, New York, New York. Made exact duplicates of the Colt Navy percussion model. Colt sued for infringement of patent and won the case, forcing them out of business.

Metzger, J. about 1725. Made flintlock Kentucky rifles at Lancaster, Pennsylvania. A rifle with his name and dated 1728 is the earliest known flintlock Kentucky rifle.

Metzger, Jacob about 1800. Flintlock musket maker at Frederick Town, Maryland. Had United States Government contract for Model 1795 flintlock muskets.

Metzger, Jacob T. 1849–1857. General gunsmith at Lancaster, Pennsylvania.

Meunier, John 1855–1886. Shop located at Milwaukee, Wisconsin. General gunsmith.

Meylin, Martin 1710–1749. Gunsmith located at West Lampeter Township, Lancaster County, Pennsylvania. Born in Switzerland, 1670.

Michlin, Edward about 1815. Flintlock Kentucky rifle maker at Halifax, Dauphin County, Pennsylvania.

Migneron, Louis about 1820. General gunsmith at 97 Main Street, St. Louis, Missouri.

Miles, John, Sr. 1776–1808. Shops located at 43 Chestnut Street and 30 South Third Street, Philadelphia, Pennsylvania. Made flintlock muskets for the Pennsylvania Militia during the Revolutionary War. Had United States Government contract and State of Pennsylvania contract for Model 1795 flintlock muskets and Army flintlock pistols. John Miles, Sr., died in 1808, and his son, John, Jr., carried on the business and moved to Bordentown, New Jersey, where he had a United States Government contract for Model 1808 flintlock muskets and Army flintlock pistols.

Miller, Abner about 1830. Flintlock Kentucky rifle maker at Easton, Pennsylvania.

Miller, Benjamin 1821–1852. General gunsmith in Berks County, Pennsylvania.

Miller, C. 1850–1870. Shop located at Honeoye, New York. Made heavy percussion hunting rifles.

Miller, David 1859–1877. General gunsmith at Troy, Ohio.

Miller, Franklin 1821–1854. General gunsmith at Reading, Pennsylvania.

Miller, George about 1820. Shop located in Columbia County, Pennsylvania. General gunsmith.

Miller, James about 1830. General gunsmith on Mason Street, Lancaster, Pennsylvania.

Miller, John 1836–1875. Shop located at Monroe, Michigan. General gunsmith.

Miller, John 1771–1782. Flintlock musket maker at Lancaster, Pennsylvania. Made arms for Pennsylvania Militia during Revolutionary War.

Miller, Mathias 1771–1788. Flintlock Kentucky rifle maker at Easton, Pennsylvania. Fine workmanship and design.

Miller, Samuel 1823–1849. General gunsmith in Lebanon County, Pennsylvania.

Miller, Samuel about 1745. Gunsmithery established at Boston, Massachusetts Bay Colony.

Miller, Samuel about 1830. General gunsmith at 30 State Street, New Haven, Connecticut.

Miller, Simon 1790–1820. Maker of flintlock Kentucky rifles and pistols at Hamburg, Pennsylvania.

Milliron, C. about 1850. General gunsmith and percussion Kentucky rifle maker at Dayton, Pennsylvania.

Mills, F. M. 1790–1814. Flintlock Kentucky rifle maker at Charlottesville, North Carolina, later moved to Harrodsburg, Kentucky. His son, Benjamin Mills, succeeded him in the business in 1814. Benjamin Mills was Assistant Armorer at Harpers Ferry Armory at the outbreak of the Civil War and went over to the Confederate States in charge of the Fayetteville Armory, North Carolina, during the War. Went back to Harrodsburg, Kentucky, and was active until 1875. Made saw-handle percussion target pistols with excellent locks and trigger action.

Milnor, Isaac about 1800. Shop located at 5 Norris Street, Philadelphia, Pennsylvania. General gunsmith.

Milnor, John about 1760. General gunsmith at Charleston, South Carolina.

Milsed, I. about 1835. General gunsmith on Main Street, Rochester, New York.

Miner, George W. about 1860. Shop located at Syracuse, New York. Made heavy caliber percussion rifles.

Minneapolis Fire Arms Co. about 1875. Plant located at Minneapolis, Minnesota. Made so-called Protector Palm Metallic Cartridge Revolver, fired by squeezing a lever against the frame holding the cylinder, holding the barrel between the index and second fingers.

Mitchell, Joseph 1820–1841. General gunsmith at Philadelphia, Pennsylvania.

Mohn, Benjamin 1835–1859. Percussion Kentucky rifle maker in Berks County, Pennsylvania.

Moisson, John 1813–1831. General gunsmith and dealer on State Street, Charleston, South Carolina.

Moll, Peter & David (Son) 1791–1835. Peter Moll, son of John Moll, established a gunshop at Hellerstown, Lehigh County, Pennsylvania. With his son David, made flintlock rifles and muskets and holster pistols used in War of 1812.

Moll, William 1740–1778. William Moll was the founder of the famous family of gunsmiths and makers of fine Kentucky rifles. All were located at Allentown, Pennsylvania. William Moll was active from 1740 to 1778. His son, John Moll, was active with him from 1748. John Moll died in 1794, leaving two sons to succeed him, John, Jr., and Peter Moll. John Moll, Jr., took over his father's shop in 1793 and was active until 1824, when his son, John Moll III took over the gunshop and was active until 1863. His son, William H. Moll, continued the business of general gunsmithing from 1863 to 1883.

Moon, C. C. & J. H. (Brothers) 1846–1854. Shop located at Martinsville, Ohio. General gunsmithing.

Moon, M. A. about 1830. General gunsmith at Buffalo, New York.

Moore, Abraham 1770–1776. Made flintlock muskets for the Pennsylvania Militia in Coventry Township, Chester County, Pennsylvania.

Moore, George 1885–1894. General gunsmith at Mt. Vernon, Ohio.

Moore, George H. about 1835. General gunsmith and dealer at 47 Queen Street, Charleston, South Carolina.

Moore, John 1803–1820. Shop located at 40 Mulberry Street, New York, New York. General gunsmith.

Moore, John about 1835. General gunsmith at 11 Beaver Street, Albany, New York.

Moore, John P. 1823–1846. Located at 302 Broadway, New York, New York. Made flintlock holster and dueling pistols and, later, percussion pistols and rifles. His son, George G. Moore, and two grandsons, Henry M. Richards and John P. Richards, carried on the business as gunsmiths and dealers at same location until 1888.

Moore Patent Firearms Co. 1862–1865. Plant at Brooklyn, New York. Made Daniel Moore patent (September 18, 1860) teat cartridge single-action revolvers. Manufacture of these was stopped by infringement proceedings by Smith and Wesson, who controlled the Rollin White patents. Later made the David Williamson patent (January 5, 1864) metallic cartridge revolvers, also all metal derringer-type cartridge pistols. Became the National Arms Company in 1865. Bought by the Colt Co. in 1870.

Moore, R. R. 1860–1870. Shop located at Seneca Falls, New York, and later Cortland, New York. Made percussion match rifles and shotguns.

Moore, William about 1860. General gunsmith at Windsor, Connecticut.

Moore, William H. about 1850. Shop located at 6 St. Paul Street, Rochester, New York. General gunsmith.

Mordecai, Joseph about 1810. General gunsmith at 4 Liberty Street, Charleston, South Carolina.

Morgan & Clapp 1864–1877. Plant located at 2 Bridge Street, New Haven, Connecticut. Made Lucius Morgan patent metallic cartridge revolvers.

Morgan, Henry about 1840. General gunsmith on Second Street, St. Louis, Missouri.

Morgan, James 1838–1848. Shop located at Utica, New York. General gunsmith.

Morgan, Joseph about 1800. General gunsmith at Morristown, New Jersey.

Morgan, Joseph about 1810. Shop located at 225 North Third Street, Philadelphia, Pennsylvania. General gunsmith.

Morlitor, Joseph 1858–1885. General gunsmith at St. Anthony, Minnesota.

Morr, A. about 1850. Percussion Kentucky rifle maker at Lancaster, Pennsylvania.

Morrett, L. 1847–1851. General gunsmith on Friend Street, Columbus, Ohio.

Morrill, Mossman & Blair 1836–1840. Henry A. Morrill, Silas Mossman, and Charles Blair. Plant at Amherst, Massachusetts. Make Elgin patent combination cutlass and percussion pistol.

Morrison, S. about 1850. Made percussion Kentucky rifles at Milton, Pennsylvania.

Morrow, Abraham 1781–1798. Shop located at 191 Chestnut Street, Philadelphia, Pennsylvania. Had United States Government contract for flintlock rifles for Pennsylvania Militia rifle companies. Name stamped on some pieces "Murrow."

Morse, George W. 1856–1888. Invented a breech-loading percussion carbine at Worcester, Massachusetts, October 28, 1856, and a soft metal cartridge which did not prove practical. During the Civil War, he gave his services to the Confederate States and in 1861 was Superintendent of the Tennessee Armory at Nashville, Tennessee. With the approach of Federal troops, he moved the equipment and machinery to Atlanta, Georgia, in 1862 and in 1863 to Columbia, South Carolina, until 1865 when the plant was destroyed by Federal cavalry. He returned to Washington, D. C., after the War and attempted to enter a claim against the government for infringement of his patent on all breech-loading arms made during the War. This claim was dismissed. He was the nephew of Samuel F. B. Morse, inventor of the telegraph. George W. Morse died in Washington, D. C., March 8, 1888.

Morse, Thomas 1866–1890. General gunsmith at Lancaster, New Hampshire.

Moses, M. A. 1860–1865. Made heavy caliber percussion rifles at Malone, New York.

Mosser, D. about 1850. Made percussion Kentucky over-and-under rifles at Danville, Pennsylvania.

Moster, George 1771–1779. Flintlock musket maker at Lancaster, Pennsylvania.

Mount Joy Forge 1742–1809. Located at Mount Joy, Pennsylvania, and after the Revolutionary War became the United States Government Arsenal at Valley Forge, Pennsylvania.

Mowery, James D. 1860–1865. Plant located at Norwich, Connecticut. Had United States Government contract for Model 1861 Springfield percussion rifles.

Moyer, George about 1820. Flintlock Kentucky rifle maker at Lancaster, Pennsylvania.

Muir & Co., William 1861–1865. Plant located at Windsor Locks, Connecticut. Had United States Government contract for Model 1861 Springfield percussion rifles.

Mulholland, James 1861–1865. Had United States Government contract for Model 1861 Springfield percussion rifles. Plant located at Reading, Pennsylvania.

Mullen, Joseph about 1770. Gunsmith at Salem, North Carolina Colony.

Mullin, Patrick & John 1841–1875. Two brothers who immigrated to the United States from Ireland, having been gunsmiths in London and Dublin. Established themselves first in a shop on Fulton Street, New York, New York, and then moved to larger quarters at 36 Maiden Lane, New York, New York. Patrick specialized in percussion shotguns; John, in percussion rifles.

Mulloy, N. P. 1866–1871. General gunsmith at Worcester, Massachusetts.

Munson, H. about 1845. Shop located at Second and Liberty Streets, Pittsburgh, Pennsylvania. General gunsmith.

Munson, Theophilus 1697–1747. Established a gunsmithery on the site of Elm and High Streets, New Haven, Connecticut Colony.

Munz, Jacob 1858–1867. General gunsmith at 133 Griswold Street, Detroit, Michigan.

Murphy & O'Connell 1857–1861. General gunsmith and dealer at 54 Chatham Street, New York, New York. Made percussion rifles and shotguns and derringer-type pistols.

Murray, J. P. 1856–1865. J. P. Murray was successor to the partnership of **Happoldt & Murray** at 45 Broad Street, Columbus, Georgia, making percussion hunting rifles and percussion pistols. During the Civil War he was Superintendent of the **Greenwood and Gray Armory**, making Confederate arms under government contract. Among these were the Murray percussion carbine, and this Armory produced some of the finest firearms made by the Confederate States.

Musgrave, S. about 1850. General gunsmith at Ironton, Ohio.

Myer, Henry 1771–1778. Made flintlock muskets for the Pennsylvania Militia, location in Pennsylvania not known.

Myer, Philip about 1850. General gunsmith at 130 Fulton Street, Pittsburgh, Pennsylvania.

NOTES

Nash, Thomas about 1640. Gunsmith at New Haven, Connecticut Colony. Armorer for the Town and Colony Militia.

Nashville Gun Factory 1861–1862. Had contract with the Confederate States Government for Model 1841 percussion Mississippi-type rifles. Closed in 1862 with the arrival of Federal troops.

Nason, C. F. 1863–1868. General gunsmith at Lewiston, Maine.

Nauman, Jacob about 1815. Shop located at Lancaster, Pennsylvania. General gunsmith.

National Arms Co. 1865–1869. Plant located at Brooklyn, New York. Took over the Moore Firearms Co. and made the Daniel Moore Patent (September 18, 1860) teat cartridge revolvers. Later made the David Williamson Patent (January 5, 1864) teat cartridge revolvers. Also, made "National" metallic cartridge derringer-type pistols.

Neal, William & John (Son) 1845–1878. Shop located at Harlow and State Streets, Bangor, Maine. Made percussion underhammer pistols and rifles.

Neave, T. about 1850. Percussion Kentucky rifle maker at Cincinnati, Ohio.

Neel, George 1849–1854. General gunsmith at Uniontown, Ohio.

Neider, A. O. about 1860. Made percussion rifles at Melrose, Massachusetts. Later moved, under the name of Neider Rifle Company, to Dowagiac, Michigan.

Neihard, Peter 1785–1793. General gunsmith and maker of flintlock Kentucky rifles. Shop located in Whitehall Township, Lehigh County, Pennsylvania.

Nelson, Alexander about 1775. Shop located at Philadelphia, Pennsylvania. Had contract with Virginian Colony Militia for flintlock muskets.

Nelson, Roger 1857–1861. General gunsmith at Medina, Ohio.

Nepperhan Firearms Co. 1859–1869. Plant located at Yonkers, New York. Made percussion revolvers similar to Colt pocket and belt models. Firm closed by Colt patent lawsuit in 1869.

Nestle, Frederick about 1850. Shop located at Baltimore, Maryland. Made percussion holster and dueling pistols.

Newbecker, Philip about 1815. General gunsmith at Halifax, Dauphin County, Pennsylvania.

Newbury Arms Co. 1855–1860. Plant located at Albany, New York. Made percussion revolvers under the Frederick D. Newbury patent dated March 20, 1855.

Newcomb, H. W. 1865–1870. General gunsmith at Eastport, Maine.

Newcomer, Abraham 1771–1775. Flintlock Kentucky rifle maker at Lancaster, Pennsylvania.

Newcomer, John about 1770. General gunsmith in Hempfield Township, Lancaster County, Pennsylvania.

Newhardt, Peter & Jacob 1774–1821. Flintlock Kentucky rifle makers at Allentown, Pennsylvania.

New Haven Arms Co. 1857–1867. Took over the Volcanic Repeating Arms Co. and was owned by Oliver F. Winchester, principle stockholder, and B. Tyler Henry, patentee of the Henry Magazine Repeating Rifle (October 16, 1860). Gave up the manufacture of volcanic pistols and manufactured the Henry lever-action magazine rifle, which later became the famous Winchester rifle. Plant located at New Haven, Connecticut, 1857 to 1866. Moved to Bridgeport, Connecticut, 1866 to 1867, when the company was reorganized under the name of the **Winchester Repeating Arms Co.**

Newton, E. M. 1858–1868. General gunsmith at Skowhegan, Maine.

Newton, Philo S. 1842–1875. General gunsmith and dealer at 72 State Street, Hartford, Connecticut. Made percussion rifles, pistols and shotguns.

Nichols & Childs 1838–1845. Rufus Nichols and Edward Childs patented (April 24, 1838) and made percussion revolving rifles and revolvers in which the cylinder revolved by a mechanism on outside of frame. Shop located at Conway, Massachusetts.

Nichols, Jonathan about 1800. Shop located at Vergennes, Vermont. Had United States Government contract for Model 1795 flintlock muskets.

Nicholson, James about 1810. General gunsmith at 177 Meeting Street, Charleston, South Carolina.

Nicholson, John 1774–1792. Shop located at Front Street, Philadelphia, Pennsylvania. Had contract for flintlock muskets for the Pennsylvania Militia. Also, dealer to ship trade of flintlock blunderbusses and pistols and cutlasses.

Nipes, Abraham about 1800. Flintlock Kentucky rifle maker in Longswamp Township, Berks County, Pennsylvania.

Nippes, Daniel & Albert S. (Son) 1808–1848. General gunsmithery at Mill Creek near Philadelphia, Pennsylvania. Had United States Government contract for Model 1840 flintlock muskets and later made percussion sporting rifles.

Nixon, Austin about 1835. General gunsmith on Washington Street, Buffalo, New York.

Noe, Bartholomew about 1840. Shop located at 172½ Bowery, New York, New York. General gunsmith.

Norman, John about 1760. General gunsmith on King Street, Charleston, South Carolina.

Norman, William about 1855. Shop located in Brooklyn, New York. General gunsmith.

Norris, S. 1862–1865. Samuel Norris with W. T. Clement had State of Massachusetts contract for Model 1863 percussion muskets for Massachusetts Militia during Civil War. Plant located at Springfield, Massachusetts. These arms were marked "S.N. & W.T.C. MASS."

Norris, William 1841–1854. General gunsmith in Brown County, Ohio.

North & Savage 1856–1860. Henry S. North and Edward Savage made percussion sliding cylinder revolvers under the H. S. North patent of June 17, 1856, at Middletown, Connecticut. The firm was succeeded by the **Savage Revolving Firearms Co.**

North, Simeon 1794–1852. Simeon North was born at Berlin, Connecticut, on July 13, 1765, and was the sixth generation of descendents of John North, who arrived from England in 1635 and settled in Farmington in the Massachusetts Bay Colony. On June 10, 1795, Simeon North purchased land on Spruce Creek, Berlin, Connecticut, and set up a forge and mill for making scythes. He probably became interested in gun making from his neighbor, Elias Beckley, who had a gunsmithery at Beckley Quarter about a mile away. North's first United States Government contract was dated March 9, 1799, for 500 flintlock horse, or dragoon, pistols known as the Model of 1799: length over-all, 14¾ inches; length of barrel, 9 inches; caliber .69; brass mountings. Marked on lock plate "S. North Berlin Con" with spread eagle over "U. States." Before the first contract was completed, he entered into his second contract, dated February 6, 1800, for 1500 pistols of the same model. Delivery was completed on both contracts September 11, 1802.

North's third government contract, dated June 30, 1808, was for 2000 Navy flintlock pistols known as Navy Model 1808. Length over-all was 16¼ inches; length of barrel, 10⅛ inches; caliber .64; iron belt hook and brass mountings. Lock plate markings same as Army Model of 1799. This contract was increased another 1000 pistols, same model, under date of December 4, 1810. In 1811, North entered a working agreement with his brother-in-law, Elisha Cheney, a clock maker, to finish screws and pins used in his pistols. Also in 1811, he was elected Lieutenant Colonel of the Sixth Connecticut Regiment and thereafter known as Colonel North. His fifth contract, dated sometime in July 1812 (records lost in Washington, D. C. due to the burning of the Capitol) was for 2000 horse, or dragoon, flintlock pistols Model 1810: length over-all, 15 inches; length of barrel, 8⅝ inches; caliber .69; iron mountings; lock plate marked same as previous models.

After the Declaration of War with England, June 18, 1812, the government urged Colonel North to expand his plant, and he moved to Middletown, Connecticut, where he built a larger plant with more water power.

North's sixth contract, dated April 16, 1813, was for 20,000 Model 1813 horse or dragoon flintlock pistols to be delivered over a period of five years. This model of 1813 was 15¼ inches over-all; length of barrel, 9 inches;

caliber .69; and iron mountings. The markings on the lock plate were "S. North" over spread eagle with "U." and "S." on either side of the eagle and below "MIDLᵀᴺ CONN." (This was the first marking showing two n's in Connecticut.) These are the first models marked Middletown and the first application of the principle of interchangeable parts. The specifications of this contract were changed on January 8, 1816. The caliber was reduced from .69 to .54 and a brass foresight was added on the forward barrel-stock band; no other changes. According to available records, 1150 were delivered with caliber .69 and the balance of 18,850 were caliber .54.

The seventh North government contract was dated July 21, 1819, for 20,000 (10,000 pairs) of horse, or dragoon, flintlock pistols to be delivered at the rate of 4000 (2000 pairs) per year. This was known as the Model of 1819. The over-all length was 15⅜ inches; length of barrel, 10⅛ inches; caliber .54; the first model with the swivel ramrod and safety catch slide on hammer, brass foresight on the barrel, and iron mountings. The delivery was as follows: 2000 in 1820, 7000 in 1821, 8000 in 1822 and 3000 in 1823, the entire contract delivered to the government 14 months in advance of final delivery date. On most of these arms the year delivered was stamped on the butt end of the lock plate behind the hammer. The other markings on the lock plate were the same as previous model. This was the last Army pistol contract Colonel North received. His eighth and last pistol contract was for Navy flintlock pistols, dated November 16, 1826, for 1000 pistols. These were known as the Navy Model 1826 and were 13¼ inches over-all; length of barrel, 8⅝ inches; and caliber .54; swivel ramrod and iron mountings, brass foresight on barrel. These pistolˢ did not have the safety slide catch on the hammer. The stampings on the lock plate were changed to "U.S." over "S. North," no spread eagle and no location of manufacture, but these were made at Middletown, Connecticut. This contract was duplicated twice, first on December 12, 1827, and again August 18, 1828. These were each for 1000 pistols, making a total of 3000 Navy flintlock pistols. These pieces carried the year made 1826 or 1827 or 1828 stamped on the lock plate behind the hammer.

While Simeon North was in Washington, D. C., in March, 1823, he made a proposal to the Ordnance Department for the manufacture of rifles. This proposal culminated in his first rifle contract, dated December 10, 1823, for 6000 rifles to be delivered at the rate of 1200 each year for five years. This was the standard Army Model of 1822 muzzle-loading flintlock rifle: 51¼ inches over-all; length of barrel, 36 inches; caliber .54; patch box on stock. Marked on lock plate "U.S." over "S. North" and year of manufacture after the hammer on lock plate. Deliveries were 1440 in 1824, 1620 in 1825, 1440 in 1826 and 1500 in 1827; thus the contract was completed one year earlier than stipulated.

North's second rifle contract was an extension of his first rifle contract and dated July 22, 1828, for the same Army model to be delivered in one year, which was done.

His third rifle contract was dated December 15, 1828, and was for 5000 Harpers Ferry Model Hall breech-loading flintlock rifles to be delivered at the rate of 1000 rifles per year over a five year period. This breech-loading rifle was 52½ inches over all, had a length of barrel of 32½ inches and the depth of chamber in receiver was 2⅜ inches, caliber .54. This rifle was marked on the top of the receiver "U.S." over "S. North Middletn Conn"

and the year of make under the above.

In 1833, while the above contract was being fabricated, Colonel North received a contract for speedy delivery of 1000 carbines for dragoons. These were Hall flintlock breech-loaders and were 45 inches over-all, with a barrel length of 26 inches. Depth of chamber in receiver was 2⅜ inches, caliber .54, also a ramrod bayonet extending 21½ inches. Markings on top of receiver same as the breech-loading rifles. The first delivery of these carbines was made in January 1834 and completed in May of the same year.

On January 27, 1835, North received another rifle contract for 4000 Hall breech-loading flintlock rifles, same specifications as previous rifle contract.

Simeon North received four more carbine contracts dated November 23, 1835, January 6, 1836, June 20, 1836, and May 22, 1839, totaling 12,500 stands of arms. These were shorter in length than the initial flintlock carbine and had no ramrod bayonets. Also, some changes were made in the lever operating the breech receiver. These carbines had a length over-all of 40 inches, a barrel length 21 inches, and markings on top side of receiver same as previous carbines and rifles with year of manufacture. These were the last of North's flintlock arms.

In February, 1843, when Colonel North was in Washington, D. C., he submitted to the Ordnance Department a new model breechblock for the breech-loader, which was later to be known as "North's Improvement." This improvement had a side lever for raising the breech. It was more easily handled and also gave a closer contact between breech and barrel. This was accepted on February 18, 1843, and the last carbine contract of May 22, 1839, was changed to include the new type of breechblock lever. 6000 carbines had been delivered to date on the old contract. The patent covering the "North Improvement" was issued July 30, 1844, jointly to Simeon North and Edward Savage, and North paid Savage a royalty to cover the joint patent. North was instructed by the Ordnance Department to proceed on his present contract with a percussion breech-loading carbine with the "North Improvement," and 500 were delivered in the latter half of 1843 and 2500 before July 1, 1846. These percussion breech-loading carbines were 40 inches over-all and had a barrel length of 21 inches, caliber .54, markings on top of receiver same as previous pieces with year of manufacture. The above contract evidently was extended, for on July 11, 1848, Colonel North recommended to the Ordnance Department the change from iron barrels to cast steel, which was authorized. On February 5, 1850, North received his last United States contract for 3000 carbines, same specifications as previous contract.

During North's career as a firearms maker, he made many presentation pieces with gold mountings and engravings. Notable among these were a pair of cased flintlock pistols for Commodore Isaac Hall and Commodore McDonough.

Simeon North died at Middletown, Connecticut, in 1852 in his 87th year, and the business was closed.

Norwich Arms Co. 1861–1869. Plant located at Norwich, Connecticut. Had United States Government contract for Model 1861 Springfield percussion rifles. Also made metallic cartridge revolvers.

Nunnemaker, Abraham 1779–1783. Flintlock Kentucky rifle maker in York County, Pennsylvania.

Nutt, Rollin 1848–1854. General gunsmith at Eagleville, Ohio.

Nutting, Ebenezer 1722–1745. Gunsmith at Falmouth (now Portland), Maine.

NOTES

Oakes, Samuel about 1800. General gunsmith at Philadelphia, Pennsylvania.

Oberholzer, Christian 1775–1778. Made flintlock muskets for the Pennsylvania Militia at Lancaster, Pennsylvania.

Oblinger, David 1859–1890. General gunsmith at Piqua, Ohio. His son, Walter, carried on the shop after his father's death in 1890 until 1892.

Oblinger, S. 1869–1879. Shop located at Troy, Ohio. General gunsmith.

O'Connell, Daniel 1855–1861. General gunsmith and dealer at 54 Chatham Street, New York, New York. Name changed to **Murphy & O'Connell,** 1857 to 1861. Made percussion rifles and shotguns and derringer-type pistols.

O'Dell, S. about 1855. General gunsmith and dealer at Natchez, Mississippi. Made derringer-type percussion pistols.

Odlin, John 1671–1685. Gunsmith at Boston, Massachusetts Bay Colony.

Offrey, P. about 1855. General gunsmith at 173 Chartres Street, New Orleans, Louisiana.

Ogden, W. E. about 1850. General gunsmith at Oswego, New York.

Oldham, Thomas about 1845. General gunsmith and percussion Kentucky rifle maker in St. Clair Township, Bedford County, Pennsylvania.

Olenhousen, Jacob about 1845. Shop located at Denwiddie near Pittsburgh, Pennsylvania. General gunsmith.

Oliver, John about 1810. Shop located at 37 George Street, Baltimore, Maryland. General gunsmith.

Olmsted, M. L. about 1860. General gunsmith at 9 North Street, Auburn, New York.

Ong, E. 1773–1777. General gunsmith at Philadelphia, Pennsylvania.

Orcutt, Samuel about 1810. General gunsmith at 51 Prince Street, Boston, Massachusetts.

Orr, Hugh 1737–1798. Born in Scotland in 1717, emigrated to the Massachusetts Bay Colony and settled at Bridgewater. Established a general gunsmithy and made flintlock muskets for the Massachusetts Militia. He died in 1798. His son, Robert Orr, learned his trade with his father and was Master Armorer of the Springfield (Massachusetts) Armory in 1795.

Orr, James 1830–1860. General gunsmith in Belmont County, Ohio.

Orton, John about 1795. Shop located on Front Street, Philadelphia, Pennsylvania. General gunsmith.

Orwin, John about 1790. General gunsmith at Carlisle, Cumberland County, Pennsylvania.

Osborn, Lot 1772–1777. Made flintlock muskets for the Connecticut Militia at Waterbury, Connecticut.

Osborne, H. 1815–1830. Shop located at Springfield, Massachusetts. Had United States Government contract for Model 1821 flintlock muskets.

Osgood Gun Works 1870–1880. Plant located at Norwich, Connecticut. Made metallic cartridge revolvers.

Oswan, Frederick 1810–1816. General gunsmith at Harpers Ferry, Virginia (now West Virginia).

Overbaugh, C. E. about 1880. Gunsmith and dealer at 300 Broadway, New York, New York. Specialized in metallic cartridge match or target rifles.

Owens, E. G. 1877–1880. General gunsmith at Denver, Colorado.

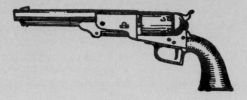

NOTES

Pachard, William M. 1854–1862. General gunsmith on the Public Square at Elyria, Ohio. Made percussion hunting rifles.

Packson, about 1635. Established a gunsmithery on Kent Island, Maryland Colony.

Page, Allen William about 1805. General gunsmith at 108 Maiden Lane, New York, New York.

Page, John 1770–1777. Shop located at Preston, Connecticut. Made flintlock muskets for the Connecticut Militia.

Palm, Jacob 1759–1777. Flintlock Kentucky rifle maker at Lancaster, Pennsylvania, 1759 to 1768, then moved to Esopus, New York, 1768 to 1777.

Palmer, Asa about 1775. Made flintlock muskets for the Connecticut Militia, location of shop not known.

Palmer, H. F. 1862–1867. General gunsmith at Adrian, Michigan.

Palmer, Thomas 1773–1776. Shop located on Market Street between Fourth and Fifth Streets, Philadelphia, Pennsylvania. Made flintlock muskets for the Pennsylvania Militia.

Palmer, William R. 1863–1865. Lived in New York, New York. Patented, on December 22, 1863, a bolt-action carbine. These were made at E. G. Lamson & Co., Windsor, Vermont, under United States Government contract and were the first bolt-action metallic cartridge arms to be approved by the United States Army.

Palmeteer, J. 1835–1860. Shop located at Poughkeepsie, New York. Made percussion rifles and pistols.

Palmetto Armory 1852–1865. Owned by Glaze and Boatwright, plant at Columbia, South Carolina. Made percussion pistols, muskets, and rifles for State of South Carolina. With the secession of South Carolina from the Union in 1861, the ownership of the Armory changed to William Glaze & Company and under government contract with the Confederate States repaired and converted to percussion rifles, muskets, and pistols. The Armory was destroyed by Federal troops in 1865.

Pannabecker, Daniel about 1825. Flintlock Kentucky rifle maker in Lancaster County, Pennsylvania.

Pannabecker, James & Jesse 1833–1861. Made flintlock and, later, percussion Kentucky rifles at Middle Creek, Lancaster County, Pennsylvania.

Pannabecker, Jefferson 1790–1810. Shop located at Hopeland, Lancaster County, Pennsylvania. Made flintlock Kentucky rifles.

Pannabecker, John 1863–1866. General gunsmith at Adamstown, Pennsylvania.

Pannabecker, Samuel 1780–1825. Flintlock Kentucky rifle maker at Allentown, Pennsylvania.

Pannabecker, William, Sr. & Jr. 1800–1880. Made flintlock and, later, percussion Kentucky rifles at Mohnton, Berks County, Pennsylvania. After his father's death in 1845, William, Jr., carried on the business at Mohnton, Pennsylvania, until 1860. He then moved to Trenton, New Jersey, from 1860 to 1865, when he moved back to Mohnton, Pennsylvania, and was active until his death in 1880.

Park, John 1878–1882. General gunsmith at Williamsburg, Clermont County, Ohio.

Parker, A. about 1850. Shop located at Ludlow, Vermont. General gunsmithing and percussion hunting rifles.

Parker, Henry about 1775. Flintlock Kentucky rifle maker at Liverpool, Pennsylvania.

Parker, Samuel about 1775. Shop located at Philadelphia, Pennsylvania. Made flintlock muskets for the Pennsylvania Militia.

Parker, Snow & Co. 1860–1868. Owned and operated by Charles Parker. Plant located at Meriden, Connecticut. Had United States Government contract for Model 1861 percussion rifles. Three sons of Charles Parker carried on the business after his death under the name of **Parker Bros.** (Wilbur, Charles, Jr., and Dexter Parker) from 1868 to 1890. Made the Parker shotgun.

Parkhill, Andrew 1778–1785. General gunsmith on Dock Street, Philadelphia, Pennsylvania.

Parsons, G. 1857–1860. Shop located at Plattsburg, New York. General gunsmith.

Parsons, Hiram about 1820. General gunsmith at Baltimore, Maryland.

Patchin, H. M. about 1860. Made percussion pistols and rifles at Springfield, Illinois.

Patton, R. F. 1858–1865. General gunsmith at Quincy, Ohio.

Patton, William 1858–1868. Shop located at Springfield, Massachusetts. General gunsmith.

Paul, James about 1800. General gunsmith at Horsham Township, Montgomery County, Pennsylvania.

Paulsley, Christian about 1810. Shop located in West Pennsboro Township, Cumberland County, Pennsylvania. General gunsmith.

Payne, S. L. about 1850. General gunsmith at Erie, Pennsylvania.

Peabody, Henry O. 1862–1870. The Peabody breech-loading action was invented by Henry O. Peabody of Boston, Massachusetts, and filed under United States Patent No. 35947, dated July 22, 1862. The arm was manufactured and controlled by the Providence Tool Co. of Providence, Rhode Island. Marshal F. Benton of New York city was also interested financially and took over the representation to the government. It was not until January 1865 that the rifle and carbine were tested by a United States Army Ordnance Board at the Springfield Armory at Springfield, Massachusetts. A number of breech-loading system models were submitted to this Board, and after preliminary tests for strength, accuracy and penetration, four systems survived, including Peabody's. Then started the tests of actual field service. The carbine and rifle were exposed to variable weather for ten days and drenched with water daily, allowed to rust, and then covered with sand and dirt. The arms were then dried suddenly at high temperatures and used in firing tests with heavy powder charges: first, a 60-gram powder charge and 3 balls each weighing 450 grains; next, with an 80-gram powder charge and 5 balls. The Peabody rifle was the only one that survived this test. Then the Peabody was tried with 120-gram powder charge and 5 balls, and still it did not burst. The Board under Major T. S. Laidley, Ordnance Department, recommended the Peabody carbine and rifle for military service. During this time the Civil War was over and on July 12, 1866, General A. B. Dyer, Chief of Ordnance, stated, "The necessity for immediate selection of a model having ceased to exist with the termination of hostilities, further action is suspended."

However, the State of Connecticut National Guard decided on breech-loaders after the war, and in competition with a number of other breech-loading actions, Peabody's was awarded the contract. The Peabody carbine was .50 caliber, and the Peabody rifle was .433 caliber, both rimfire metallic cartridge.

Peacock, Thomas about 1750. Established gunsmithery at Charleston, South Carolina Colony.

Peard, Thomas L. about 1850. General gunsmith at 7 North Street, Hartford, Connecticut.

Pearson, James about 1775. Made flintlock muskets for Pennsylvania Militia at Philadelphia, Pennsylvania.

Pecare & Smith Firearms Mfg. Co. 1847-1861. (Jacob Pecare and Josiah Smith.) Plant located at 180 Center Street, New York, New York. Made percussion pepperboxes of fine workmanship. Some cased presentation pieces.

Peck, A. about 1800. Shop located at Hartford, Connecticut. Had United States Government contract for Model 1795 flintlock muskets.

Peck & Bowman 1860-1864. Plant located at Atlanta, Georgia. Had Confederate States contract for percussion muskets and rifles.

Peebles, Robert about 1775. Shop located in Cumberland County, Pennsylvania. Made flintlock muskets for the Pennsylvania Militia.

Peloux, about 1820. Maker of flintlock rifles at Philadelphia, Pennsylvania.

Pence, Jacob about 1770. Fintlock Kentucky rifle maker in Earl Township, Lancaster County, Pennsylvania.

Penhallow, John about 1730. Gunsmith at Boston, Massachusetts Bay Colony.

Pennsylvania Gun Works 1776-1779. Established February 1776 by the State of Pennsylvania in Philadelphia, Pennsylvania, for the manufacture of flintlock muskets. With the approach of the British Army on Philadelphia, the equipment and personnel were moved to Valley Forge in December 1776. In September 1777 the plant was moved to Reading, Pennsylvania. Early in 1779 the works were closed by order of the State of Pennsylvania.

Pennypacker, Daniel 1772-1808. Made flintlock Kentucky rifles in Berks County, Pennsylvania. Active from 1772 to 1808, when his son, William, carried on the business as a general gunsmith until 1858.

Percival, Orville 1840-1850. Inventor of the Percival magazine percussion pistol at Moodus, Connecticut. These were made by H. Smith & Co., Norwich, Connecticut.

Perkin, Joseph 1781-1803. General gunsmith on Water Street, Philadelphia, Pennsylvania. In 1803 he became Master Armorer at Harpers Ferry Armory.

Perkins & Coutty about 1780. Shop located at Second and Spruce Streets, Philadelphia, Pennsylvania. Made flintlock long arms and pistols.

Perkins, James, Luke & Rufus (Brothers) 1800-1813. Shop located at Bridgewater, Massachusetts. Had United States Government contract for Model 1795 and later Model 1808 flintlock muskets.

Perrein, Dennis about 1800. General gunsmith in Philadelphia, Pennsylvania.

Perry & Goddard 1860-1868. General gunsmiths and dealers in New York, New York. Agents for C. Sharps four-barrel metallic cartridge pistols.

Perry, Horatio B. 1857–1868. General gunsmith at Salem, Massachusetts.

Perry, H. V. 1840–1870. Made percussion pepperboxes and percussion match rifles at Jamestown, New York.

Perry, J. 1877–1880. General gunsmith at Del Norte, Colorado.

Perry Patent Arms Co. 1853–1857. Alonzo D. Perry patented January 16, 1855, the Perry breech-loading percussion mechanically primed carbines, rifles and pistols. Plant located at Newark, New Jersey. Some of the carbines were purchased by the United States Navy.

Peterman, Abraham 1852–1875. General gunsmith at 205 Dock Street and later 131 Walnut Street, Philadelphia, Pennsylvania. Made percussion shotguns of fine workmanship and design.

Pettingill, C. S. 1856–1862. Patented a double-action hammerless percussion revolver at New Haven, Connecticut, July 22, 1856. These were made by Rogers & Spencer, Willowdale (near Utica), New York. Some were purchased by the United States Government for Army and Navy issue.

Pfloeger, William & John (Son) about 1850. Percussion Kentucky rifle makers in Allegheny Township, Allegheny County, Pennsylvania.

Pheatt, Gideon K. 1859–1884. General gunsmith at 189 Summit Street, Toledo, Ohio. His two sons, D. G. and F. A. Pheatt, carried on the business at this location from 1884 to 1896.

Phelps, Silas 1770–1777. Shop located at Lebanon, Connecticut. Made flintlock muskets for the Connecticut Militia.

Philippi, Samuel 1821–1877. General gunsmith and flintlock and, later, percussion Kentucky rifle maker at Easton, Pennsylvania. His son, Solomon, entered the shop with him in 1865.

Phillips, E. about 1860. Made heavy caliber percussion rifles. Shop located at New York, New York.

Phillips, James about 1830. General gunsmith at 79 Westminster Street, Providence, Rhode Island.

Phips, James 1643–1663. Established a gunsmithery on the Kennebec River in Massachusetts Bay Colony.

Pickel, Henry 1800–1811. Flintlock Kentucky rifle and flintlock musket maker at York, Pennsylvania. Had contract with State of Pennsylvania for flintlock muskets for Pennsylvania Militia.

Pieper, Abraham about 1800. General gunsmith at Lancaster, Pennsylvania.

Pierce, Henry about 1850. Shop located at Liverpool, Ohio. Made heavy caliber percussion hunting rifles.

Pierson, Silas about 1820. General gunsmith at 23 Oak Street, New York, New York.

Pike, Samuel about 1845. Shop located at Brattleboro, Vermont. General gunsmith.

Pim, John about 1720. Established a gunsmithery on Anne Street, Boston, Massachusetts Bay Colony. Also imported flintlock fowling pieces and pistols.

Piper, S. about 1850. General gunsmith at Oswego, New York.

Pipino, Jacob about 1855. Shop located at Baltimore, Maryland. General gunsmith.

Plank, William about 1820. General gunsmith at Greenwood Township, Columbia County, Pennsylvania.

Plant Mfg. Co. 1860–1866. Owned by E. H. Plant and A. H. Plant at New Haven, Connecticut. Made metallic cartridge revolvers under the Willard C. Ellis patents (July 12, 1859) and the N. White patents (July 21, 1863), assigned to the Plant Mfg. Co. Merwin & Bray, New York, New York, acted as their agents and distributors. Had United States Government contract for Army revolvers.

Plate, A. J. 1849–1871. General gunsmith and dealer on Leidesdorff Street, San Francisco, California. Moved to 103 Commercial Street in 1855 and to 411 Sansome Street in 1864.

Pleasants & Chanley about 1800. Made cased flintlock dueling pistols at Philadelphia, Pennsylvania.

Plushel, F. 1866–1870. General gunsmith at Cedar Falls, Iowa.

Pole, Edward about 1775. Shop located on Market Street, Philadelphia, Pennsylvania. General gunsmith.

Pollock, S. about 1840. General gunsmith at New Castle, Pennsylvania.

Pomeroy, Eltweed 1630–1671. Eltweed Pomeroy, founder of the Pomeroy dynasty of gunmakers in America, was a gunsmith in Devonshire, England, and emigrated to America in 1630. He set up a gunsmithery at Dorchester, Massachusetts Bay Colony, where he was active from 1630 to 1635. He then moved to Windsor, Connecticut Colony, and established a gunsmithery from 1635 to 1670. He moved to Northampton, Massachusetts Bay Colony, in 1670 and died in 1671. Eltweed Pomeroy had two sons, Medad and Eldad. Medad, born 1637, went in his father's shop in 1659 at Windsor. He moved with his father to Northampton in 1670. He was an active gunsmith until his death December 30, 1716. Eldad worked for his father at Windsor and died in Boston in 1662.

Medad had a son, Ebenezer, born May 30, 1669, who was apprenticed to his father in the Northampton gunsmithery and carried on the trade until his death January 27, 1754. Ebenezer Pomeroy was a captain in the Massachusetts Colony Militia from 1704 to 1713. Ebenezer had a son, Seth, who carried on the gunshop at Northampton. Seth had a son, Lemuel, who also carried on the business at Northampton and was active in the political affairs of the Colony. His son, Lemuel, Jr., succeeded his father in the business at Northampton and in 1800 moved to Pittsfield, Massachusetts. He established a gunshop there on East Street. In 1808 he had contracts for flintlock muskets for the Massachusetts Militia and on June 20, 1816, received his first United States Government contract for 5000 Model 1816 Army flintlock muskets. In January 1817 the Springfield, Massachusetts, Armory delivered to him the two pattern flintlock muskets. The Army Model 1816 flintlock musket had an over-all length of $57^{11}/_{16}$ inches; barrel, 42 inches; caliber .69; stock, black walnut; mountings, browned finish. The markings on lockplate were "U.S." over year of make behind the hammer and in center of lockplate "L. Pomeroy" under spread eagle. His second flintlock musket contract was dated May 17, 1823, for 10,000 Model 1816 flintlock muskets, same specifications as above, to be delivered at the rate of 2000 a year for five years. Pomeroy's next government contract was dated February 26, 1835, for 6000 Army flintlock muskets Model 1835 to be delivered over a period of five years at 1200 per year. The Model 1835 had an over-all length of $57^{13}/_{16}$ inches; barrel, 42 inches; caliber .69. The brass pan had a fence, the stock was black walnut, and the mountings had bright finish. The lockplate was marked same as previous model with the year of manufacture behind the hammer. On

March 18, 1842, Pomeroy received a contract for 1000 additional muskets as above. On September 10, 1846, all of the muskets under contract had been delivered. Lemuel Pomeroy died August 25, 1849, thus ending the name of Pomeroy as firearms makers.

Pond, Lucius W. 1859–1870. Shop located at Worcester, Massachusetts. Made top-break metallic cartridge revolver which was declared an infringement on Smith and Wesson patents. Later, to overcome infringement, made a front-loading cylinder revolver with removable steel shells.

Pool, Lemon about 1870. General gunsmith at Springfield, Ohio.

Pooley, James about 1860. Shop located at Memphis, Tennessee. General gunsmith.

Porter & Fitchitt about 1840. Shop located at Philadelphia, Pennsylvania. Made percussion pistols.

Porter, Patrick W. 1845–1851. Shop located at New York, New York. Made percussion pistols and rifles. He was killed by backfire explosion while demonstrating one of his pieces to Samuel Colt.

Ports, J. A. 1870–1882. General gunsmith at Sunbury, Ohio.

Post Self Acting Pistol Co. about 1850. Owned by J. Post and plant at New Haven, Connecticut. Made double-action percussion pepperboxes.

Potts, William 1880–1884. General gunsmith at Columbus, Ohio.

Poultney & Trimble 1857–1875. Plant located at 200 West Baltimore Street, Baltimore, Maryland. Made Gilbert Smith patent (June 23, 1857) percussion breech-loading carbine, under United States Government contract.

Pounds, I. 1843–1855. Maker of percussion rifles and shotguns at Columbus, Ohio.

Powell, Palemon 1839–1856. General gunsmith and dealer on Walnut Street, Cincinnati, Ohio. The name was carried on through three generations, at the above address. **Powell & Brown,** 1856 to 1858. **P. Powell,** 1858 to 1870. **Powell & Son,** 238 Main Street, 1870 to 1891, and **Powell & Clement,** 1891 to 1908.

Poyas, Francis D. 1825–1840. General gunsmith at 17 Meeting Street, Charleston, South Carolina. Made cased flintlock dueling pistols of excellent workmanship and design.

Poyas, James about 1810. Shop located at 84 Meeting Street, Charleston, South Carolina. General gunsmith. Probably father of Francis D. Poyas.

Prahl, Lewis 1775–1790. Shop located in Philadelphia, Pennsylvania. Made flintlock muskets for the Pennsylvania Militia.

Prailish, Charles about 1855. General gunsmith at Lancaster, Pennsylvania.

Pratt, Alvan 1835–1868. Born Sherborn, Massachusetts, November 23, 1790. Established a general gunsmith shop at Concord, Massachusetts, in 1835 and was active until 1868. Known for the accuracy and workmanship of his handmade percussion match rifles. Died at Concord, Massachusetts, January 20, 1877.

Pratt, Elisha 1847–1854. General gunsmith at Marietta, Ohio.

Pratt, G. D. about 1855. Shop located at Attica, New York. Made percussion match rifles.

Pratt, Henry 1832–1875. General gunsmith at Roxbury, Massachusetts,

1832 to 1861. Then moved to 116 Dudley Street, Boston, Massachusetts, 1861 to 1875.

Prescott, E. A. 1860-1874. Plant located at Worcester, Massachusetts. Made metallic cartridge revolvers and had United States Government contract for Navy revolvers. Later sued by Smith and Wesson for patent infringement.

Price, Joseph about 1800. General gunsmith at 498 North Second Street, Philadelphia, Pennsylvania.

Price & Moore about 1800. General gunsmithery at 6 Peck Slip, New York, New York.

Pringle, John 1775-1779. Made flintlock muskets for the Pennsylvania Militia at Philadelphia, Pennsylvania.

Prissey, Elias 1855-1874. Shop located at Hooversville, Pennsylvania. Made Kentucky and target percussion rifles.

Protector Arms Co. about 1870. Plant located at Philadelphia, Pennsylvania. Made metallic cartridge revolvers.

Providence Tool Co. 1860-1880. Plant located at Providence, Rhode Island. Had United States Government contract for Model 1861 percussion rifles. Also, made the Peabody patent (July 22, 1862) breech-loading cartridge carbines and rifles. The government contract for the carbines was canceled due to the ending of hostilities of the War between the States, and the carbines were purchased by the Connecticut State Militia. Peabody carbines and rifles were also sold to foreign governments.

Provost, about 1760. General gunsmithery at Old Slip, New York, New York.

Putnam, Enoch 1775-1780. Shop located at Granby, Massachusetts. Made flintlock muskets for the Massachusetts Militia.

NOTES

Quackenbush, H. M. 1871–1882. Made small caliber metallic cartridge target rifles at Herkimer, New York.

Quinby, Dennis 1864–1868. General gunsmith at Northfield, Vermont. Made percussion rifles.

Quinnebaug Rifle Co. about 1850. Plant located at Southbridge, Massachusetts. Manufactured underhammer percussion rifles and pistols.

NOTES

Raaf, Jacob about 1820. Flintlock Kentucky rifle maker at Halifax, Dauphin County, Pennsylvania.

Radcliffe, T. W. 1858–1864. General gunsmith, dealer, and importer at Columbia, South Carolina. Sold English-made percussion revolvers to the Confederate States.

Radcliffe, William 1865–1875. Shop located at Middletown, Connecticut. General gunsmith.

Rader, Wesley 1855–1880. General gunsmith at Chillicothe, Ohio.

Raffsnyder, John 1779–1785. Maker of flintlock Kentucky rifles at Reading, Pennsylvania.

Raker, Charles about 1850. General gunsmith in Bedford County, Pennsylvania.

Ramage & Carrier 1875–1881. Shop located at Trinidad, Colorado. General gunsmithing.

Ramsdell & Neal 1868–1878. Charles V. Ramsdell and John Neal, general gunsmiths at Harlow Street, Bangor, Maine. In 1878 the partnership was dissolved. The firm of Charles V. Ramsdell and J. W. Ramsdell moved to State Street, Bangor, Maine, 1878 to 1890.

Randall, Thomas C. about 1800. Made flintlock Kentucky rifles at Lancaster, Pennsylvania.

Ransior, J. L. about 1790. General gunsmith at 210 King Street, Charleston, South Carolina.

Ransom, James 1776–1778. General gunsmith at Halifax, North Carolina. Also master armorer of the Colony Armory at Halifax, North Carolina.

Rappahannock Forge 1775–1781. On the Rappahannock River at Falmouth, three miles from Fredericksburg, Virginia. Established by Act of the Assembly of Virginia, June 1775. Purchased by the Colony from the **Hunter Iron Works**. Made flintlock muskets and pistols for the Virginia Militia. Closed in December 1781.

Rathfong, Frederick 1770–1772. Flintlock Kentucky rifle maker at Conestoga, Pennsylvania.

Rathfong, George 1774–1819. Born at Lancaster, Pennsylvania, in 1750. Established a general gunsmithery at Lancaster, Pennsylvania, in 1774. In 1776, entered the Continental Army serving as an armorer until 1801, when he returned to Lancaster and was active as a flintlock Kentucky rifle maker until his death in 1819.

Rathfong, Jacob 1810–1839. Flintlock Kentucky rifle maker at Marietta, Lancaster County, Pennsylvania.

Raub, William 1860–1871. General gunsmith on Third Avenue, New York, New York.

Rauber, Frederick about 1730. Established a gunsmithery in Berks County, Pennsylvania.

Raymond & Robitaille 1856–1862. Edward A. Raymond and Charles Robitaille, located at Brooklyn, New York, were co-patentees (July 27, 1858) with C. S. Pettingill patent (July 22, 1856) hammerless percussion Army and Navy revolvers. These were made under United States Government contract at **Rogers & Spencer** at Willowvale, New York.

Raymond, William 1858–1865. General gunsmith at Winona, Minnesota.

Raynes, about 1860. Made heavy caliber percussion rifles at New York, New York.

Reach, C. H. about 1880. General gunsmith at Marshall, Michigan.

Read, Robert & William 1775–1802.
Made flintlock muskets for the Maryland Militia at Chesterton, Maryland.

Read, William about 1805. General gunsmith at 11 Water Street, Baltimore, Maryland.

Read, William 1826–1852. General gunsmith at Boston, Massachusetts. Name changed to **William Read & Son** at 107 Washington Street, Boston, Massachusetts, 1852 to 1870.

Rector, Charles A. 1845–1861. General gunsmith and dealer at 3 East Genesee Street, Syracuse, New York.

Reddick, about 1775. General gunsmith at Baltimore, Maryland.

Reece, J. N. 1884–1889. General gunsmith and dealer at Springfield, Massachusetts.

Reed, Joseph 1770–1800. Shop located at Lancaster, Pennsylvania. General gunsmith.

Reid, James 1862–1868. General gunsmith and dealer at 167 East 26th Street, New York, New York in 1862. Moved to 171 East 26th Street, New York, New York, 1863 to 1865. Then moved to Catskill, New York, 1865 to 1868. Made percussion and metallic cartridge revolvers and derringer-type pistols, also "knuckle-duster" revolvers.

Reid, Templeton about 1825. General gunsmith at Milledgeville, Georgia.

Rein, John 1863–1875. Shop located on Bowery, New York, New York. Made percussion and metallic cartridge target and match rifles.

Reincke, Frederick about 1845. General gunsmith at 242 North Eighth Street, St. Louis, Missouri.

Reinhart, Peter A. 1853–1896. Shop located at Loudenville, Ohio. Noted for fine workmanship and accuracy of percussion and metallic cartridge match and target rifles.

Reiter, Leonard about 1800. Flintlock Kentucky rifle maker in Berks County, Pennsylvania.

Remington, Eliphalet 1816–1861. Eliphalet Remington made his first flintlock rifle in his father's forge at Ilion, New York, in 1816. From this interest in gunsmithery grew the Remington firm. By 1829, he had developed considerable business in custom-made flintlock rifles, shotguns and pistols, and in 1845 he received his first United States Government contract for 5000 Harpers Ferry percussion rifles and in 1846 a United States contract for Jenks percussion carbines. In 1856, his sons, Philo, Samuel, and Eliphalet, Jr., became partners in the new firm of E. Remington & Sons and, in 1857, announced the first Remington percussion revolvers. These were under the Fordyce Beal patent of June 24, 1856, and followed by two improved models. In 1860, they brought out the first Remington-Beal's single-action percussion Army and Navy model revolvers. Eliphalet Remington, Sr., died at Ilion, August 12, 1861, and Philo took over management of the partnership. Also, in 1861, they made the first models of Riders Patent (August 17, 1858) pocket double-action percussion revolvers, and this was followed by the Remington-Rider single-shot derringer, patented September 13, 1859. Then followed a series of United States Government contracts for the Remington Army and Navy models single-action percussion revolvers. The first double-action of these models was produced in 1863. In 1865, the corporation of E. Remington and Sons was set up succeeding the partnership. The company brought out, in 1866, a single-action revolving rifle which was not successful and less than 3000 were made. After the Civil War, Remington looked to the foreign markets and advertised a complete line of percussion revolvers, rifles, muskets, carbines, shotguns, repeating pistols, rifle canes, and revolving rifles. In 1867, orders came in from France, Denmark, Sweden, Spain and Egypt. The first of Remington's metallic cartridge models, brought out in 1861, was the Zig-Zag derringer, the patent of William H. Elliott (May 29, 1860). These were not practical, and less than a thousand were manufactured. Following these in 1863 were the famous double action Remington-Elliott derringer in both .22 (5 shots) and .32 caliber (4 shots). These proved to be a popular arm and were manufactured until 1888. The next model to be brought out for metallic cartridge was the Vest Pocket single-action pistol in 1865. In 1866, Remington received a United States Government contract for the single-shot "rolling block" Army and Navy model pistols. These were .50 caliber rim-fire and, later, center-fire cartridges. A target pistol of this model was also made in .22 caliber. Also in 1866, Remington brought out the double barrel (over-and-under) derringer. These were .41 caliber rim fire. In 1867, these were also made as a single barrel pistol. Rider received a patent August 15, 1871, for a magazine pistol. The magazine was under the barrel and fed by spring pressure to the chamber. This was put on the market late in 1871, but it did not have a popular sale. In 1874, Remington brought out what was known as the New Line Revolver. This was under the patent of W. S. Smoot (October 21, 1873) and, with improved models, was manufactured until 1888. These were .32 and .38 caliber center and rim fire. The United States Government gave Remington a contract in 1874 for the Model 1875 Army Revolver and in 1889 for the Model 1890 Army Revolver, both .45 caliber. In December 1882, Samuel Remington died, and

Philo bought his stock interest and became the largest stockholder. In 1886, the company went into a receivership and in 1888 was reorganized as the **Remington Arms Company.** Philo Remington died in April 1889.

Remington, George H. about 1860. Shop located at 53 Dominick Street, Rome, New York. General gunsmith.

Remley, John H. about 1855. General gunsmith at Lancaster, Pennsylvania.

Rendyles, Bernard about 1850. Shop located at Steubenville, Ohio. General gunsmith.

Renker, Rudolph about 1855. General gunsmith at Lancaster, Pennsylvania.

Renwick, E. S. about 1860. Shop located at New York, New York. Made Perry and Goddard patents (June 21, 1864) metallic cartridge derringer-type two-shot pistol.

Resor, Jacob about 1815. Shop located on Front Street, Cincinnati, Ohio. Made flintlock Kentucky rifles.

Resor, Peter 1775–1781. Flintlock Kentucky rifle maker at Lancaster, Pennsylvania.

Reuthe, F. 1854–1860. General gunsmith at New Haven, Connecticut.

Revol, J. R. 1850–1880. General gunsmith and dealer at New Orleans, Louisiana. Made percussion dueling pistols of fine workmanship.

Reynall, Richard about 1800. General gunsmith at 56 Water Street, Baltimore, Maryland.

Reynolds, Francis 1844–1865. General gunsmith and dealer at 48 Chatham Street, New York, New York.

Rheiner, William 1858–1867. Shop located at 63 Randolph Street, Detroit, Michigan. General gunsmith.

Rhodes, William about 1800. Had United States Government contract for Model 1795 flintlock muskets at Providence, Rhode Island.

Richards, John about 1795. General gunsmith at Savannah, Georgia.

Richards, L. B. 1825–1835. Shop located at Lynchburg, Virginia. General gunsmith.

Richardson, Joel 1816–1825. General gunsmith at North Street, Boston, Massachusetts.

Richardson, John about 1840. Shop located at Rutland, Vermont. General gunsmith.

Richardson, O. A. 1857–1865. Shop located at Lowell, Massachusetts. Made percussion match and target rifles of heavy caliber. During the Civil War, these were much in demand as sharpshooters' arms. In 1865, the name was changed to Richardson & Cutter at 66 Central Street, Lowell, Massachusetts, until 1868.

Richardson & Overman 1860–1866. Had United States Government contract for the Gallager Patent (July 17, 1860) percussion breech-loading and, later, metallic cartridge carbines. Plant located at Philadelphia, Pennsylvania.

Richwine, C. about 1840. Flintlock and later percussion Kentucky rifle maker at Reading, Pennsylvania.

Rickets, John 1859–1883. General gunsmith at Mansfield, Ohio.

Ricks, Thomas 1677–1681. Gunsmith at Boston, Massachusetts Bay Colony.

Riddle, about 1770. Maker of flintlock Kentucky rifles at Lancaster, Pennsylvania.

Rider, Nathaniel 1840–1857. Made saw-handle underhammer percussion pistols at Southbridge, Massachusetts.

Rife, Charles about 1855. General gunsmith at Cincinnati, Ohio.

Rigdon & Ansley & Co. 1864–1865. Charles H. Rigdon and Jesse A. Ansley succeeded the partnership of Leech and Rigdon and moved to Marbury Street, Augusta, Georgia, and carried on the Confederate States Government contracts for an iron frame copy of Colt Model 1851 percussion Navy revolvers.

Riggins, Thomas 1845–1865. General gunsmith in McMinn County, Tennessee. Noted for his fine workmanship on flintlock and, later, percussion Kentucky match and squirrel rifles. In 1862, moved to Knoxville, Tennessee, and became an armorer in the Confederate Army.

Riggs, B. about 1850. General gunsmith at Bellows Falls, Vermont.

Riggs, Joseph 1775–1780. Shop located at Derby, Connecticut. Made flintlock muskets for the Connecticut Militia.

Riley, Edward 1816–1820. General gunsmith at Cincinnati, Ohio.

Riley, William L. 1849–1854. Shop located at Watertown, Ohio. General gunsmith.

Ringle, Mathias about 1840. Made percussion Kentucky rifles at Blairsville, Pennsylvania.

Ripley Bros. about 1840. General gunsmiths at Windsor, Vermont.

Ripley, John B. about 1835. Shop located at Claremont, New Hampshire. General gunsmith.

Rittenhouse, Benjamin 1775–1779. Shop located at Nottingham, Chester County, Pennsylvania. Made flintlock muskets for the Pennsylvania Militia.

Ritter, Jacob 1775–1783. General gunsmith at Philadelphia, Pennsylvania.

Ritzel, P. M. 1830–1850. Maker of flintlock and, later, percussion Kentucky rifles in Starke County, Ohio.

Road, M. L. about 1860. General gunsmith at Marshall, Michigan.

Robbins, C. about 1870. Shop located at New York, New York. General gunsmith.

Robbins, Kendall & Lawrence 1844–1857. (Samuel E. Robbins, N. Kendall, and Richard S. Lawrence.) Plant located at Windsor, Vermont. Made percussion ring-trigger pepperboxes from 1844 to 1846, when Kendall withdrew from the firm and it became Robbins & Lawrence, continuing at Windsor, Vermont, 1846 to 1857. In 1852, they also built a plant at Hartford, Connecticut, which they sold in 1856. Their first United States Government contract was dated January 5, 1848, for Model 1841 percussion rifles. Later they received government contracts for Jennings Patent (December 26, 1849) percussion rifles and Sharps Patent (September 12, 1848) breech-loading percussion carbines.

Robbins, W. E. about 1860. Shop located at Manesburg, Pennsylvania. Made underhammer percussion rifles.

Roberts Breech-Loading Arms Co. 1865–1874. Owned by General Benjamin S. Roberts, who held the patents (September 23, 1862) of the Roberts breech-loading percussion rifles and carbines. The offices were at 39 Broadway, New York, New York, and the arms were made under United States Government contract at the Providence Tool Co., Providence, Rhode Island.

Roberts, W. 1850–1856. Shop located at Danville, New York. Made percus-

sion pepperbox type of both short and long arms.

Roberts, William about 1840. General gunsmith at 43 Main Street, Rochester, New York.

Robertson, W. about 1840. General gunsmith at Philadelphia, Pennsylvania. Noted for cased dueling percussion pistols, some saw-handle.

Robinson Arms Manufactory 1860–1864. Owned by Samuel C. Robinson. Plant located at Richmond, Virginia. Under Confederate States Government contract made breech-loading percussion carbines after the Sharps model. These were poorly made, and the plant was taken over by the Confederate Government in 1863, and muzzle-loading carbines were fabricated. The Confederate Government moved the plant equipment to Tallassee, Alabama, in 1864.

Robinson, Edward 1863–1865. Had United States Government contract for Model 1861 percussion rifles at New York, New York.

Robinson, John about 1845. General gunsmith at Ninth Street, St. Louis, Missouri.

Robinson, W. S. 1857–1867. Shop located at Mt. Clemens, Michigan. General gunsmith.

Robson, James O. 1852–1870. General gunsmith at 139 Main Street, Buffalo, New York. Made percussion hunting rifles.

Rocketer, J. H. about 1850. Shop located at Syracuse, New York. General gunsmith.

Rodier, Lewis C. 1853–1873. General gunsmith at Springfield, Massachusetts.

Roesser, Mathias & Peter (Brothers) 1739–1782. Gunsmithery at Lancaster,

Pennsylvania. One of the earliest known Pennsylvania flintlock Kentucky rifle makers. Peter had a son, William, who dropped the double s, spelling the name **Roeser**. William carried on the shop at Lancaster, Pennsylvania, until 1808.

Roessler, Frederick about 1855. General gunsmith at 20 St. Phillip Street, Charleston, South Carolina.

Rogers, John & Charles (Brothers) 1809–1846. General gunsmiths at 7 North Second Street, 1809 to 1810, then at 52 High Street, Philadelphia, Pennsylvania, 1810 to 1846. Made flintlock Kentucky rifles and flintlock holster pistols. In 1814, they bought the Valley Forge Iron Works at Valley Forge, Pennsylvania, converting it to a gunsmithery, and had United States Government contract for Model 1816 flintlock muskets.

Rogers, L. 1868–1879. General gunsmith at Xenia, Ohio.

Rogers, R. 1847–1866. Had a general gunsmithery at Utica, New York, 1847 to 1850, when the name was changed to **Rogers & Hearst**, 1850 to 1861. During this period some pill lock pistols were made. In 1861, the name was changed to **Rogers & Spencer**, and the plant moved to Willowvale, New York (about five miles south of Utica, New York). Here, under United States Government contract, were made the Pettingill (patent January 4, 1859) hammerless percussion revolver, the Freeman (patent December 9, 1862) percussion revolver and the Rogers & Spencer (H. S. Rogers patent November 4, 1862) percussion revolver.

Roll, F. X. about 1840. General gunsmith at Liberty, Missouri.

Rood, Morgan L. 1851–1875. General gunsmith at Marshall, Michigan, 1851 to 1866, when he moved to 202 Fifteenth Street, Denver, Colorado, where he was active until 1875. Made percussion hunting and "Plains" rifles.

Roop, John 1770–1775. Flintlock Kentucky rifle maker at Allentown, Pennsylvania.

Root, E. K. 1855–1870. General gunsmith at Bristol, Connecticut.

Roper, J. 1836–1848. General gunsmith at 51 South Second Street, 1836 to 1841, and at 98 North Third Street, St. Louis, Missouri, 1841 to 1848.

Roper, Sylvester H. 1866–1895. General gunsmith at Amherst, Massachusetts, from 1866 to 1889, when he incorporated under the name of the **Roper Repeating Rifle Co.** from 1889 to 1895. Made repeating metallic cartridge rifles and carbines under the S. H. Roper patent dated April 10, 1876.

Ropp, Adam about 1850. General gunsmith at Lancaster, Pennsylvania.

Rose, Ludwic about 1845. Shop located at 80 Catherine Street, New York, New York. General gunsmith.

Ross, Benjamin about 1820. General gunsmith at Portland, Maine.

Ross, Boone about 1850. Shop located at Terre Haute, Indiana. Made heavy caliber percussion rifles.

Ross, Elijah about 1810. General gunsmith at Zanesville, Ohio.

Ross, Samuel about 1850. Shop located at 12 Fifth Street, Pittsburgh, Pennsylvania. General gunsmith.

Roth, Charles 1858–1875. General gunsmith at Wilkes-Barre, Pennsylvania. Made heavy caliber percussion rifles. His son, E. F. Roth, was active with him from 1870 to 1875.

Roth, George 1841–1847. General gunsmith and percussion Kentucky rifle maker at Heidelberg Township, Lebanon County, Pennsylvania.

Rowe, Webster 1859–1868. General gunsmith at Skowhegan, Maine.

Rowell, H. H. about 1875. General gunsmith and dealer at Sonora, California.

Royet, Louis 1858–1889. Emigrated from France to the United States in 1858 and established a general gunsmithery at Reading, Pennsylvania.

Rudolph, A. E. 1875–1880. General gunsmith at Canon City, Colorado.

Rugart, Peter about 1770. Flintlock Kentucky rifle maker at Lancaster, Pennsylvania.

Ruggles, A. about 1855. Shop located at Stafford, Connecticut. Made underhammer percussion pistols and rifles.

Ruggles, F. about 1825. General gunsmith at Hardwick, Maine.

Rupertus Patent Pistol Mfg. Co. 1858–1888. Company founded by Jakob Rupertus at 120–122 North Sixth Street, Philadelphia, Pennsylvania. Started as a manufacturer of percussion pepperboxes, patented July 19, 1864,

and then developed into the manufacture of small caliber metallic cartridge revolvers. Some of the brand names of the revolvers were "Terrier," "Hero," and "Empire."

Rupp, John & Herman 1775–1784. Makers of flintlock Kentucky rifles and flintlock holster pistols at Lancaster, Pennsylvania.

Ruppert, William about 1775. General gunsmith and flintlock musket maker at Lancaster, Pennsylvania.

Rush, William 1769–1771. General gunsmith on High Street, Philadelphia, Pennsylvania.

Rusily, Jacob 1782–1822. Flintlock Kentucky rifle maker at Lancaster, Pennsylvania.

Ryan Pistol Mfg. Co. about 1870. Owned by Thomas E. Ryan. Office and sales room on Franklin Street, New York, New York. Plant located at Norwich, Connecticut. Made small caliber metallic cartridge revolvers under the brand names of "Retriever" and "Napoleon."

Rynes, Michael about 1770. General gunsmith in Lancaster County, Pennsylvania.

NOTES

Sackett, D. S. about 1860. Maker of percussion pistols and rifles at Westfield, Massachusetts.

Saget, J. 1867–1877. General gunsmith, importer, and dealer in New Orleans, Louisiana. Designed and patented, in June 1872, a metallic cartridge revolver. These were made for him in Belgium. Also, patented a .22 caliber metallic cartridge pistol that was part of and concealed in the handle of a walking stick.

Saltonstall, Gurdon 1762–1775. Made flintlock muskets for the Connecticut Militia. Location of shop not known.

Samples, Betherel 1818–1854. Flintlock and later percussion rifle maker at Urbana, Ohio.

Sanborn, Charles about 1850. General gunsmith at Concord, New Hampshire.

Sanderson, M. F. 1855–1860. Percussion rifle maker at Proctorsville, Vermont.

Sargent, Charles R. about 1850. General gunsmith at 43 Merrimack Street, Newburyport, Massachusetts.

Sarson & Roberts 1863–1866. J. B. Sarson and William S. Roberts located at 11 Platt Street, New York, New York. Had United States Government contract for Model 1861 percussion rifles.

Savage, Edward 1856–1866. Shop located at Middletown, Connecticut. Became the Savage Revolving Firearms Co., 1860 to 1866. Made the H. S. North patent (June 17, 1856) percussion Navy revolver under United States Government contract. Also, made Model 1861 percussion rifles.

Savage, James about 1810. General gunsmith at Baltimore, Maryland.

Savage Arms Co. 1895 to date. Founded by Arthur W. Savage at Utica, New York. Made sporting and military rifles and carbines. Became Savage Arms Co., 1898 to 1915, and Savage Arms Corp., 1915 to date.

Sawyer, Joshua W. about 1845. General gunsmith at Portland, Maine.

Saylor, Jacob 1779–1790. Shop located in Bedford County, Pennsylvania. Made flintlock rifles and muskets.

Schalck, Chris 1825–1870. General gunsmith at Williamsport, Pennsylvania.

Schalck, George 1860–1892. General gunsmith at 13 Norwegian Street, Pottsville, Pennsylvania.

Scheaner, William 1779–1790. Flintlock Kentucky rifle maker at Reading, Pennsylvania.

Schelling, Frederick & Peter (Brothers) about 1855. Percussion Kentucky rifle makers at Lancaster, Pennsylvania.

Schenkle, J. P. 1850–1857. General gunsmith at Boston, Massachusetts.

Schirer, John 1806–1830. General gunsmith and dealer at Charleston, South Carolina. Shop located at 177 Meeting Street, 1806 to 1819; at 188 Meeting Street, 1819 to 1825; and at 48 Queen Street, 1825 to 1830.

Schley, Jacob about 1775. Shop located at Frederickstown, Maryland. Made flintlock rifles and muskets for the Maryland Militia.

Schmidt, Heinrich about 1855. General gunsmith and percussion Kentucky rifle maker at Lancaster, Pennsylvania.

Schnader, Frank 1839–1852. Shop located in Berks County, Pennsylvania. General gunsmith.

Schnaut, T. G. 1822–1838. General gunsmith at Monmouth, New Jersey.

Schneeloch, Otto 1868–1878. Shop located at 109 Ewen Street, Brooklyn, New York. General gunsmith.

Schneider, F. A. about 1870. General gunsmith and dealer at Columbia, South Carolina.

Schneider & Glassick 1859–1862. William S. Schneider and Frederick G. Glassick gunsmiths and dealers at 20 Jefferson Street, Memphis, Tennessee. Later had Confederate States Contract for the manufacture of copies of Colt Army models.

Schneider, M. 1848–1866. General gunsmith at Dayton, Ohio, became Schneider & Son (Edward J. Schneider) 1866 to 1877.

Schoener, Henry 1850–1863. General gunsmith at Reading, Pennsylvania.

Schontz, P. H. 1860–1865. Shop located at Fulton, Ohio. General gunsmith.

Schooler, Thomas about 1810. General gunsmith at Charleston, South Carolina.

Schorer, Andrew about 1780. Flintlock Kentucky rifle maker at Bethlehem, Pennsylvania.

Schrapel, Louis 1875–1880. General gunsmith at Georgetown, Colorado.

Schrayer, George about 1810. Shop located at Franklin Street, Baltimore, Maryland. General gunsmith.

Schreidt, John 1758–1777. Flintlock Kentucky rifle maker at Reading, Pennsylvania.

Schroeder, H. 1850–1863. General gunsmith at Bloomington, Indiana. Patented (December 23, 1856) a percussion breech-loading carbine. A few of these were purchased by the Ordnance Department, United States Army.

Schroyer, Mathias about 1800. Shop located at Taney Town, Maryland. Had United States Government contract for Model 1795 flintlock muskets.

Schryer, George 1758–1770. Flintlock Kentucky rifle maker at Reading, Pennsylvania.

Schryer, George about 1810. General gunsmith on Hookstown Road, Baltimore, Maryland.

Schubarth, Casper D. 1861–1868. Shop located at 84 Weyhosset Street, Providence, Rhode Island. Had United States Government contract for Model 1861 percussion rifles.

Schuler, J. R. about 1850. General gunsmith at Liverpool, Pennsylvania.

Schweitzer, Abram 1805–1823. Flintlock Kentucky rifle maker at Chambersburg, Pennsylvania.

Schweitzer, C. 1863–1866. General gunsmith at Canton, Ohio.

Scott, John about 1740. General gunsmith and dealer at corner of Broad and Church Streets, Charleston, South Carolina Colony.

Scott, Sylvester about 1850. Shop located at Bristol, Vermont. General gunsmith.

Scott, William J. & Richard H. (Brothers) 1848–1861. Makers of percussion rifles and pistols at 9 Beaver Street, Albany, New York.

Seaver, E. about 1840. General gunsmith at Vergennes, Vermont.

Secor, O. P. 1867–1871. Shop located at Peoria, Illinois. General gunsmith

Seeley, J. about 1870. Made heavy caliber percussion rifles at Reedsburg, Wisconsin.

Seeley, T. B. about 1865. Made percussion rifles and shotguns at Dunkirk, New York.

Seiple, Christian about 1805. General gunsmith and flintlock Kentucky rifle maker at Lancaster, Pennsylvania.

Selden, A. about 1875. Shop located at Whitehall, New York. Made percussion hunting rifles and shotguns.

Seldon, A. about 1845. General gunsmith at Dorset, Vermont.

Sell, Jacob about 1795. Flintlock Kentucky rifle maker at York, Pennsylvania.

Sells, Benjamin 1835–1865. Flintlock and, later, percussion Kentucky rifle maker at Georgetown, Ohio.

Sells, F. N. 1860–1885. General gunsmith at Laurel, Ohio.

Sells, Michael 1827–1860. Shop located at Augusta, Kentucky. General gunsmith.

Selvridge, John 1800–1830. Flintlock Kentucky rifle maker in Bradley County, Tennessee. Moved to Cleveland, Ohio, in 1826, active until 1830.

Sensey, J. about 1855. General gunsmith at Chambersburg, Pennsylvania.

Sever, Joseph & Shubabel 1775–1782. Makers of flintlock muskets for the Massachusetts Militia at Framingham, Massachusetts.

Seward, Benjamin 1796–1803. General gunsmith and dealer on Adams Street, Boston, Massachusetts.

Shaffer, Baltzer about 1785. General gunsmith at Baltimore, Maryland.

Shakanoosa Arms Works 1862–1864. Under Confederate States Government contract made percussion rifles and carbines at Rome, Georgia. Moved to Adairsville, Georgia, and then to Dawson, Georgia, where the plant was destroyed by Federal troops.

Shannon, William & Hugh 1807–1816. Had United States Government contract for Model 1808 flintlock muskets. Shop located at 24 Passyunk Street, Philadelphia, Pennsylvania.

Sharpless, Daniel about 1775. Made flintlock muskets for the Pennsylvania Militia at Philadelphia, Pennsylvania.

Sharps, Christian 1848–1874. Christian Sharps was born at Washington, New Jersey, in 1811, and was living in Cincinnati, Ohio, in 1848 when he filed his first application for patents on the falling breechblock type of breechloading rifle. He established a plant at Mill Creek, Pennsylvania, where the first rifles were made in 1850. In 1851 he moved to Hartford, Connecticut, formed the **Sharps Rifle Manufacturing Co.,** and turned over the patents to this company on a royalty basis. He resigned from the company in 1853. The company continued the manufacture of breech-loading rifles and carbines and received extensive government contracts during the War between the States, when the Sharps carbine, using paper and linen cartridges, was a popular side arm for cavalry troops. The company carried on at Hartford, Connecticut, until 1874, when it was reorganized and refinanced under the name of **Sharps Rifle Company,** until it went out of business in 1881.

Christian Sharps returned to Philadelphia, Pennsylvania, and formed **C. Sharps & Company** in 1854 and manufactured pistols only. First a breechloading .38 caliber percussion pistol, using his former basic patents of the falling breechblock. This pistol was not successful, as it leaked at the breech.

He developed his reputation on a .22 and .32 caliber rim-fire metallic cartridge four-barrel pistol. This pistol had a ratchet on the hammer that revolved the firing pin by cocking and fired the four barrels in rotation. His plants were at the following addresses in Philadelphia, Pennsylvania: 336 Frankford Road, 1854 to 1856; 17th Street and Market Street, 1856 to 1857; Fairmount and North 30th Street, 1857 to 1862.

In 1862, he formed the partnership of Sharps and Hankins, continuing at Fairmont and North 30th Street, 1862 to 1866, when he dissolved the partnership and reverted back to the original name of C. Sharps & Company and moved to 24th and Green Streets, Philadelphia, Pennsylvania, 1866 to 1874. Christian Sharps died at Vernon, Connecticut, in 1874.

Shattuck Arms Co. 1880–1890. Owned by C. S. Shattuck. Plant located at Hatfield, Massachusetts. Made cartridge shotguns, pistols, and revolvers.

Shaw, Albert S. 1840–1851. General gunsmith in Morrow County, Ohio.

Shaw, Joshua 1814–1820. Born in England in 1777, emigrated to the United States and settled in Philadelphia, Pennsylvania. No records as a firearms maker, but some arms bore his name. In 1814, he developed the first nipple, or cone, and percussion cap ignition of powder system in America, first with an iron cap, then a pewter cap, and, finally, the copper cap in 1816. He was refused a United States Patent on the grounds that he was not a citizen. The percussion system was gradually used by all arms makers, and later Congress officially recognized Shaw's claim and voted him $20,000 in token of this recognition.

Shawk & McLanahan 1858–1863. Abel Shawk and J. K. McLanahan

established a shop at Carondelet outside of St. Louis, Missouri. Made revolvers after the Colt percussion model, .36 caliber, six shots, and brass frame. Failed to secure a United States Government contract and closed in 1863.

Sheets, Adam, Henry & Philip (Brothers) 1768–1780. Shop located at Shepards Town, Berkeley County, Virginia. Made flintlock muskets for the Virginia Militia and did general gunsmithing.

Shell, John about 1835. General gunsmith in Hanover Township, Dauphin County, Pennsylvania.

Shell, Martin 1757–1790. Flintlock Kentucky rifle maker in Dauphin County, Pennsylvania. His son, Martin, Jr., was with him in 1783. Martin, Sr., died in 1790, and his son carried on the shop until 1796.

Shell, Samuel 1790–1810. Flintlock Kentucky rifle maker at Liverpool, Pennsylvania. In 1808, his son, John Shell, migrated to Leslie County, Kentucky, and set up a shop there. Was active until 1830.

Shener, John & William about 1810. General gunsmiths at Reading, Pennsylvania.

Shennfeldt, N. about 1850. Made percussion Kentucky rifles at Clarion, Pennsylvania.

Shepler, Peter 1848–1854. General gunsmith at Clarks, Ohio.

Sherman, A. P. about 1850. Made heavy-caliber percussion rifles at Portsmouth, Ohio.

Sherman, Nathaniel about 1695. Established a gunsmithery at Boston, Massachusetts Bay Colony.

Sherman, William R. 1862–1869. General gunsmith at New Bedford, Massachusetts.

Sherry, John 1830–1870. Born at Lancaster, Pennsylvania, in 1797 and set up his own shop in Beaver Township, Clarion County, Pennsylvania, in 1830. Made percussion Kentucky rifles and improved rifling methods.

Shnyder, Charles about 1790. General gunsmith at Baltimore, Maryland.

Shoff, Jacob about 1790. Flintlock Kentucky rifle maker in Cavernon Township, Berks County, Pennsylvania.

Shorer, Andrew about 1775. Flintlock musket maker at Bethlehem, Pennsylvania.

Short, Biscoe & Co. 1862–1865. J. C. Short and L. N. Biscoe established a factory at Tyler, Texas. Had Confederate States Government contract for Model 1841 percussion rifles.

Shriver, John about 1795. Flintlock Kentucky rifle maker in Mt. Pleasant Township, York County, Pennsylvania.

Shryer, George about 1805. General gunsmith in Antrim Township, Franklin County, Pennsylvania.

Shuler, John 1808–1818. Shop located at Liverpool, Pennsylvania. Had United States Government contract for flintlock Army holster pistols and flintlock rifles and muskets.

Sichles, Stephen about 1825. General gunsmith on Howard Street, Albany, New York.

Siebert, Christian & Charles M. (Brothers) 1851–1886. Makers of fine percussion match and target rifles and hunting rifles. Shop located at 253 South High Street, 1851 to 1872, and at 217 South High Street, 1872 to 1886, Columbus, Ohio.

Siebert, Henry L. 1849–1858. General gunsmith and percussion rifle maker at Cincinnati, Ohio. Shop located at 279 Main Street under his name, 1849 to 1852. Under name of Griffiths & Siebert, 1852 to 1854, and under his own name, 1854 to 1858.

Siegling, W. C. 1866–1872. Made percussion rifles and shotguns. Shop located at Columbus Avenue, Sandusky, Ohio.

Sill, A. V. 1828–1835. General gunsmith on Main Street, Buffalo, New York.

Simms, R. B. about 1820. Shop located at 116 Orange Street, Brooklyn, New York. General gunsmith.

Simpson, J. about 1855. Made percussion pistols at New Britain, Connecticut.

Simpson, Paul J. about 1840. General gunsmith at 18 Spruce Street, New York, New York.

Sinclair, John 1802–1820. Flintlock Kentucky rifle maker at Lancaster, Pennsylvania.

Siple, Chris about 1810. Flintlock Kentucky rifle maker in Middletown Township, Dauphin County, Pennsylvania.

Slack, Peter 1854–1892. General gunsmith at 61 Main Street, Springfield, Ohio. In 1874, his son, A. J. Slack, was taken into the business and the name became Slack & Son until 1892.

Sleret, Englehart 1854–1860. General gunsmith on High Street, Chillicothe, Ohio.

Slocomb, Hardin 1820–1846. General gunsmith at Worcester, Massachusetts, 1820 to 1831. Moved to Homer, New York, where he was active 1831 to 1846.

Slocum, F. P. 1863–1867. Lived in Brooklyn, New York, and invented a sleeve cartridge revolver, patented

April 14, 1863. These were made by the **Brooklyn Arms Co.**

Slonaker, George about 1845. General gunsmith in Union Township, Bedford County, Pennsylvania.

Slotter & Co. 1859–1871. Owners, Charles and Henry Slotterbeck (**Slotter** a trade name). Plant located in Philadelphia, Pennsylvania. Made percussion derringer-type pistols and match and target rifles. Located first at 400 Lynd Street and later at 1528 Frankford Road.

Slotterbeck, Charles 1878–1884. Shop and dealer at San Francisco, California. Made high-grade metallic cartridge hunting and match rifles.

Small, Jacob about 1800. Flintlock Kentucky rifle maker at South Beaver Township, Allegheny County, Pennsylvania.

Small, Samuel 1849–1854. General gunsmith at New Lisbon, Ohio.

Smart, Eugene 1865–1890. Shop located at Dover, New Hampshire. General gunsmith.

Smith, Anthony 1779–1790. Flintlock rifle and musket maker at Bethlehem, Pennsylvania.

Smith, Charles W. about 1830. General gunsmith at Cherry Creek, Chautauqua County, New York.

Smith, David about 1850. Shop located at 52 Pleasant Street, Hartford, Connecticut. General gunsmith.

Smith, Dexter 1867–1875. Made breech-loading shotguns at Springfield, Massachusetts.

Smith, E. H. about 1845. General gunsmith at Manchester, New Hampshire.

Smith, G. 1857–1865. General gunsmith at Chicopee Falls, Massachusetts.

Smith, George 1850–1866. Made percussion match and target rifles and pistols at New York, New York.

Smith, J. B. about 1855. Made high-grade percussion rifles at Northfield, Vermont.

Smith, Jeremiah 1770–1779. Made flintlock muskets for the Rhode Island Militia at Lime Rock, Rhode Island.

Smith, John 1797–1801. Shop located at Rutland, Vermont. Had United States Government contract for Model 1795 flintlock muskets.

Smith, John 1866–1869. General gunsmith at Hessville, Ohio.

Smith, Johnston 1776–1780. Shop located in Northampton County, Pennsylvania. Made flintlock muskets for the Pennsylvania Militia.

Smith, Joseph about 1850. General gunsmith at 20 Church Street, Hartford, Connecticut.

Smith & Co., L. C. 1880–1888. Founded by Lyman Cornelius Smith. Plant located at Syracuse, New York. Made cartridge shotguns. Purchased by the **Hunter Arms Co.** in 1888.

Smith, Levi 1866–1869. Shop located at Clyde, Ohio. General gunsmith.

Smith, Lewis 1855–1859. General gunsmith at Tiffin, Ohio.

Smith, Martin about 1815. General gunsmith at Lancaster, Pennsylvania.

Smith, Martin about 1830. Shop located at Greenfield, Massachusetts. General gunsmith.

Smith, Obadiah about 1810. General gunsmith in Brunswick County, Virginia.

Smith, Otis A. 1873–1890. Made metallic cartridge revolvers under Smith patent dated April 15, 1873. Shop located at Brook Falls, Connecticut.

Smith, Patrick 1861–1875. Shop located at 127 Main Street, Buffalo, New York. Made percussion and metallic cartridge rifles.

Smith, Perley about 1845. General gunsmith at Lyman, New Hampshire.

Smith, Thomas about 1800. Shop located on Broad Street, New York, New York. General gunsmith.

Smith & Wesson 1851 to date. Horace Smith and Daniel Baird Wesson formed a partnership. Based on Horace Smith's patent, dated August 23, 1851, and with improvements bought from B. Tyler Henry filed a patent (February 14, 1854) under the name of Smith and Wesson for a metallic cartridge repeating magazine pistol and rifle. Their plant was established at Norwich, Connecticut, and they manufactured the "Volcanic" pistol. The **Volcanic Repeating Arms Co.** was incorporated in July 1855, and Smith and Wesson turned over their patent rights to this company. Oliver F. Winchester bought control of the **Volcanic Repeating Arms Co.** and moved the plant to New Haven, Connecticut, in February 1856.

With the expiration of the Colt's patents in the latter part of 1856, Smith and Wesson established a plant at Springfield, Massachusetts, on May 1, 1857, for the manufacture of metallic cartridge revolvers.

Smith, William 1849–1854. General gunsmith at St. Marys, Ohio.

Sneider, Anthony about 1775. Flintlock rifle and musket maker at Lancaster, Pennsylvania.

Sneider, Edward & C. W. 1860–1887. General gunsmiths at 214 West Pratt Street, Baltimore, Maryland.

Snell, Elijah 1820–1834. General gunsmith at Auburn, New York. His son, Chauncey, succeeded him in 1834 and was active until 1860.

Snevely, Jacob about 1815. Shop located at Harrisburg, Pennsylvania. General gunsmith.

Snively, William 1854–1865. General gunsmith at Flints Falls, Washington County, Ohio.

Snyder, Jacob about 1845. General gunsmith in Liberty Township, Bedford County, Pennsylvania.

Soleil, Francis about 1655. Established a gunsmithery at New Amsterdam (New York, New York).

Sowers, John about 1840. General gunsmith at Philadelphia, Pennsylvania.

Spangler, George about 1860. Maker of percussion Kentucky rifles at Monroe, Wisconsin.

Specht, Eley about 1850. Shop located at Beaverstown, Pennsylvania. Made percussion Kentucky rifles.

Speed, Robert 1820–1840. General gunsmith at Boston, Massachusetts.

Spencer, Christopher M. 1860–1869. Received his first patent for the Spencer Repeating rifle on March 6, 1860. Approved by an Army Ordnance Board in 1862, and United States Government contract for carbines was awarded to the **Spencer Repeating Rifle Co.** with offices on Tremont Street, Boston, Massachusetts. The carbines and rifles were made by the Burnside Rifle Co. at Providence, Rhode Island. In 1869, the **Winchester Arms Co.** purchased the patents and equipment.

Spencer, Dwight W. about 1860. General gunsmith at Hartford, Connecticut.

Sperl, H. about 1855. Made percussion hunting rifles at Susquehanna, Pennsylvania.

Spies, A. W. 1832-1860. General gunsmith and dealer at Broadway and Fulton Street, New York, New York. Became **Spies, Kissan & Co.** from 1860 to 1876 at same address.

Spiller & Burr 1861-1864. Edward N. Spiller and David J. Burr established a plant in Atlanta, Georgia, when they received from the Confederate States Government, November 30, 1861, a contract for percussion revolvers. These were patterned after the Whitney Naval model and had a brass frame. The plant was purchased and operated by the Confederate Government in February 1864 until the capture of Atlanta, Georgia, by Federal troops.

Spitzer, Sr. & Jr. 1775-1820. Made flintlock muskets for the Virginia Militia in Virginia, location of shop not known. After the Revolutionary War, Spitzer, Jr., set up a general gunsmithy at Newmarket, Virginia, and was active until 1820.

Sporleder, Louis 1867-1880. General gunsmith at Walsenburgh, Colorado.

Sprague & Marston 1849-1855. Made percussion pepperbox and single-shot pistols at New York, New York.

Sprague, Nathaniel about 1840. General gunsmith at Nashua, New Hampshire.

Springfield (Massachusetts) Armory 1795 to date. In 1777, General George Washington authorized the establishment of an arsenal and powder magazine at Springfield, Massachusetts. This was used as a recruiting post, depot for storage of military arms and supplies, and the repair of arms. In 1781, it was taken over as the Massachusetts State Armory. Pursuant to an act of Congress September 6, 1785, the Secretary of War was ordered to make a semi-annual report each year to Congress of all government arms of troops in the field, reserve arms in arsenals, mainly stored at Springfield, Massachusetts; West Point, New York; and Philadelphia, Pennsylvania. The report communicated to the Senate on December 10, 1793, showed that the reserve stocks of arms in these arsenals was 31,015 stands of arms, of which about 26,000 were complete and serviceable. On April 2, 1794, Congress authorized President Washington to establish two Federal armories and appropriated $340,000 for their establishment and the manufacture of arms. President Washington selected Springfield, Massachusetts, and Harpers Ferry (then Virginia) as the two sites. An Ordnance Board, after tests, selected the French flintlock musket, Model of 1763, made at the Royal armories at Charleville, France, as the pattern musket; and this became, with slight variations, the first United States Army flintlock musket, known as Model 1795. Congress authorized the manufacture of 7000. This musket was 59½ inches over-all; average weight, 8 pounds 14 ounces; barrel, 44⅝ inches; and .69 caliber, stock of black walnut, barrel and mountings bright finish. The markings of the lock plate were a spread eagle with "U.S." in script below, between the hammer and the frizel (frizzen) spring, with the word "Springfield" slightly curved reading from the rear stamped behind the hammer. From 1799 to 1803, the year of make was stamped on the heel of the butt plate and from 1804 appeared on the lock plate under the word "Springfield" behind the hammer.

Fabrications of these muskets started in 1795, and 245 muskets were proved and viewed that year. Alexander Crawford hand filed and completed the first gunlock. 838 were proved in 1796 and 1028 in 1797, 1044 in 1798, and 4595 in 1799. The Springfield Arsenal, also, provided pattern models for private contractors.

The second type of Springfield flintlock musket was known as the Model of 1808. This musket was 59 inches over-all; weight with bayonet, about 10 pounds; barrel, 44½ inches; caliber .69; black walnut stock; barrel and mountings, bright finish. The markings on the lock plate were changed from the previous model: the "U.S." in script is above the spread eagle and "Springfield" curved below, and the year of make is marked horizontally behind the hammer. On this model the flashpan is, also, an integral forged part of the lock plate.

From this period on, of course, all U. S. arms models have been made at the Springfield Arsenal.

Springfield Arms Co. 1851–1869. Made James Warner patent, dated January 7, 1851, percussion revolvers and, later, metallic cartridge revolvers. These infringed the Smith and Wesson patents, and the plant was closed.

Stack, John about 1805. General gunsmith in Annsville Township, Dauphin County, Pennsylvania.

Stafford, T. J. 1860–1861. Made single-shot metallic cartridge pistols under his patent, dated December 7, 1860, at New Haven, Connecticut.

Stall, Christian about 1815. Flintlock Kentucky rifle maker at Harrisburg, Pennsylvania.

Stamm, Jacob 1859–1864. General gunsmith at Sardinia, Ohio.

Stamm, Philip, Sr. & Jr. 1842–1866. Philip Stamm, Sr., a general gunsmith in Brown County, Ohio, 1842 to 1862, when he died. His son, Philip, Jr., moved to Ripley, Ohio, and was active 1862 to 1866.

Stanbra, Charles 1855–1892. General gunsmith at Creston, Iowa, from 1855 to 1865. Then moved to Bellingham, Washington, and was active until 1892.

Stannard, F. P. 1874–1882. Shop located at Janesville, Wisconsin. General gunsmith.

Stapelton, James about 1860. Percussion rifle maker in Huntingdon County, Pennsylvania.

Starr Arms Co. 1860–1868. Ebenezer Townsend Starr, second son of Nathan Starr, Jr., was born at Middletown, Connecticut, August 18, 1816. On January 15, 1856, residing in New York City, he received Patent No. 14118 for a single-action percussion revolver, caliber .54. The revolver had a removable screw on the right side of the frame, which permitted the barrel to drop on a hinge and the cylinder to be removed. He received a second patent, No. 30843, on December 4, 1861, for a double-action revolver of the same type. There were two models of this revolver: the Army model with eight-inch barrel, .44 caliber; and Navy model with six-inch barrel, .36 caliber. He formed the **Starr Arms Company** at 267 Broadway, New York, New York, and under United States Government contracts sold 47,950 of these two models to the Army and Navy during the War between the States. A greater number were Army models, as Navy models are now scarce.

The **Starr Arms Company** had two plants, one at Yonkers, New York, and one at Binghamton, New York. The company was closed in 1868.

Starr, Nathan, Sr. & Jr. 1798–1845. Nathan Starr was born at Middletown, Connecticut, April 14, 1755. On July 5, 1776, he was appointed Armorer of the Second Battalion, Colonel Francis Sages' Regiment, Connecticut Militia. Established a foundry and forge at Middletown, Connecticut, after the Revolutionary War and received his first contract from the United States Government in 1798 for 2000 Model 1798 cavalry swords. From this date until 1823, he had numerous government contracts for swords, sabers, cutlasses, artillery swords, and pikes.

Nathan Starr, Jr., was born February 20, 1784, and entered the business with his father in 1812. A son was born to Nathan Starr, Jr., on August 10, 1812, named Elihu William Nathan Starr, and he entered the business in 1837. The identification marks of the Starr family on the arms for the purpose of establishing dates are: "N. Starr & Co.," 1798 to 1808; "N. Starr," 1808 to 1837; "N. Starr & Son," 1837 to 1845.

The first United States firearms contract received was dated December 9, 1823, for 4000 Model 1817 flintlock rifles (side patch box on stock). The second contract, dated May 21, 1828, was for 5000 Model 1816 flintlock muskets. Another contract was made on October 28, 1830, for improved models of flintlock muskets, and these contracts carried on in yearly allotment basis until 1845, when private arms contracts were suspended by the government.

On May 3, 1839, Nathan Starr received a patent for a breech-loading percussion carbine. The breech-loading action was similar to the Hall breech-loader, except on this arm the opening and cocking was accomplished by an eccentric operated by a side lever. This lever action resembles the "North Improvement" on the Hall carbine. Only experimental models were made of the Starr carbine, which never went into production. The butt-stock of this carbine had a hinged lid, and in the recess in the stock were 16 tubes to hold paper or linen cartridges.

Nathan Starr, Sr., died at Middletown, Connecticut, July 29, 1821. Nathan Starr, Jr., died August 31, 1852, and Elihu W. N. Starr died June 14, 1891. The business, as arms makers, was discontinued in 1845.

Statler, William 1868–1874. Made percussion hunting rifles at Logan, Ohio.

Steel, John 1771–1787. Shop located at Boston, Massachusetts. Made flintlock muskets for the Massachusetts Militia.

Steel & Lathrop about 1860. Makers of percussion saw-handle pistols at Albany, New York.

Stein, Mathias 1868–1875. General gunsmith at Milwaukee, Wisconsin.

Stein, William 1868–1880. Shop located at 309 Federal Street, Camden, New Jersey. General gunsmith.

Steinman, John & Frederick (Son) 1810–1836. General gunsmiths in Philadelphia, Pennsylvania. Shop located on North Third Street, 1810 to 1819; on Green Street, 1819 to 1829; and on Germantown Road, 1829 to 1836.

Stenger, T. S. about 1865. General gunsmith at Waterloo, Iowa.

Stenzel 1730–1740. Maker of flintlock Kentucky rifles at Lancaster, Pennsylvania Colony.

Stephens, John about 1775. Flintlock musket maker at Philadelphia, Pennsylvania.

Sterling, R. about 1840. General gunsmith at Newburgh, New York.

Stetson, Edward about 1835. Shop located at 18 Purchase Street, New

Bedford, Massachusetts. General gunsmith.

Stevens, A. C. 1855–1875. Made percussion match and target rifles at Hudson, New York.

Stevens & Co., J. 1864–1919. Founded by Joshua Stevens at Chicopee Falls, Massachusetts. Made small caliber metallic cartridge pocket pistols and, later, rifles and single-shot target pistols. The following are the names of the company in sequence: **J. Stevens & Co.,** 1864 to 1888; **Stevens Arms & Tool Co.,** 1888 to 1904; **J. Stevens Arms Co.,** 1904 to 1919. All were located at Chicopee Falls, Massachusetts. Joshua Stevens retired from the company in 1896.

Stevens, Martin 1859–1868. General gunsmith at Stoughton, Massachusetts.

Stewart, John about 1810. Shop located at 6 Laight Street, Baltimore, Maryland. General gunsmith.

Stillman, Amos & Ethan (Brothers) 1798–1818. Shop located at Farmington, Connecticut. Had United States Government contract for Model 1795 and Model 1808 flintlock muskets.

Stinger, Thomas 1835–1850. General gunsmith in Lycoming County, Pennsylvania.

Stocking & Co. 1847–1865. Founded by Alexander Stocking at Worcester, Massachusetts. Made percussion pepperboxes and single-shot pistols. Noted for fine cased presentation pepperboxes.

Stone, David about 1800. Shop located at Walpole, New Hampshire. Had United States Government contract for Model 1795 flintlock muskets.

Story, Asa 1835–1843. Made percussion hunting rifles and shotguns at Windsor, Vermont.

Stowell, E. J. 1873–1878. General gunsmith at Brooklyn, New York.

Strohl, John 1868–1872. Shop located at Fremont, Ohio. General gunsmith.

Stronach, John about 1750. Gunsmith at Charleston, South Carolina Colony.

Strossmeister, Charles 1857–1863. General gunsmith at Cincinnati, Ohio.

Stroup, O. M. about 1880. Shop located at Wellington, Ohio. General gunsmith.

Stuart, Charles P. 1850–1870. Made percussion rifles at 43 Washington Street, Binghamton, New York.

Stull, Jerry & Samuel (Brothers) 1858–1861. General gunsmiths at Millwood, Ohio.

Sturdivant, Lewis G. 1862–1864. Had Confederate States contract, dated March 6, 1862, for the manufacture of percussion rifles. Shop located at Battle Street, Talladega, Alabama.

Sturgis, Julius about 1855. General gunsmith at Lancaster, Pennsylvania.

Sutherland, Samuel 1855–1865. General gunsmith and dealer at 174 Main Street, Richmond, Virginia, before the War between the States. Under Confederate States contract altered flintlock rifles to percussion and made percussion underhammer pistols.

Sutter, C. about 1855. General gunsmith and dealer at Selma, Alabama. Made derringer-tye percussion pistols.

Sutton, George about 1800. General gunsmith at Pittsburgh, Pennsylvania.

Swartz, Peter about 1785. Maker of flintlock muskets for the Pennsylvania Militia. Shop located in York County, Pennsylvania.

Sweet, Jenks & Son 1810–1814. Made Model 1808 flintlock muskets under United States Government contract at Pawtucket, Rhode Island.

Sweet, W. A. about 1850. Shop located at Syracuse, New York. Made percussion target pistols.

Sweigart, Adam about 1815. Flintlock Kentucky rifle maker at Halifax, Dauphin County, Pennsylvania.

Sweitzer, Charles 1864–1875. General gunsmith at Mauch Chunk, Pennsylvania.

Sweitzer, Daniel about 1810. Shop located at Millerstown, near Lancaster, Pennsylvania. Had United States Government contract for Model 1808 flintlock pistols.

Swinehart, Andrew 1846–1854. Shop located at Somerset, Ohio. General gunsmith.

Symmes, John C. 1857–1864. Shop located at Watertown, Massachusetts. Had United States Government contract for percussion breech-loading carbines under Symmes patent, dated November 16, 1858.

NOTES

Tallasse Armory 1862–1865. Confederate States Arsenal at Tallassee, Alabama. Made percussion muzzle-loading carbines and, later, percussion breech-loading carbines. Carbines marked "C. S. Tallassee Ala."

Talley 1768–1774. Shop located at Boston, Massachusetts Bay Colony. Master Armorer for the Colony.

Tanner, N. B. 1862–1864. Shop located at Bastrop, Texas. Had contract from the State of Texas for percussion rifles for Texas troops in the Confederate Army.

Tarpley, Garrett & Co. 1863–1865. Owned by Jere H. Tarpley and J. & F. Garrett. Tarpley was granted a Confederate States patent, January 14, 1863, for a breech-loading percussion carbine. With J. & F. Garrett established a plant at Greensboro, North Carolina, and made the arms under Confederate States contract.

Taylor, A. J. 1850–1858. General gunsmith, dealer, and importer at 209 Clay Street, San Francisco, California. Was killed by the accidental discharge of a pistol, September 25, 1858.

Taylor & Co., L. B. about 1870. Made metallic cartridge pistols at Chicopee Falls, Massachusetts.

Teaff, James 1849–1861. General gunsmith at Steubenville, Ohio. In 1856, his son, Nimrod, entered the business. James Teaff died in 1861, and his son was active until 1891.

Teff, George 1774–1776. Made flintlock muskets for the Rhode Island Militia. Location of shop in the Colony not known.

Tell, Frederick 1790–1820. General gunsmith at Hagerstown, Maryland.

Tennessee Armory 1861–1862. Established by the Confederate States Government at Nashville, Tennessee. Repaired old arms and converted sporting guns to military weapons. Arms marked "Tennessee Armory" after conversion. Moved to Greenville, South Carolina, when Federal troops approached Nashville. Operated only about 18 months.

Tetzel, Edmund 1882–1900. General gunsmith at Terre Haute, Indiana.

Thayer, O. G. about 1865. Made percussion target rifles at Chardon, Ohio.

Thomas, Benjamin about 1750. General gunsmith at Hingham, Massachusetts Colony.

Thomas, Horatio 1846–1854. Shop located at Higginsport, Ohio. General gunsmith.

Thomas, Isaac about 1770. Made flintlock muskets for the Maryland Militia in Harford County, Maryland.

Thomas, J. A. 1865–1868. General gunsmith at Meriden, Connecticut.

Thomas, Milton & H. (Son) about 1845. Shop located at Kingman, Illinois. General gunsmith.

Thompson, Henry about 1875. General gunsmith at Fremont, Ohio.

Thompson, J. R. about 1860. Made percussion hunting rifles at Jackson, Michigan.

Thompson, John about 1800. General gunsmith at Philadelphia, Pennsylvania.

Thompson, Samuel 1820–1825. Shop located at Columbus, Ohio. General gunsmith.

Thresher, A. about 1855. Made percussion pistols at Stafford, Connecticut.

Thurman, C. 1879–1885. General gunsmith at Larimor, Iowa.

Tidd, Marshal 1846–1860. Maker of percussion pistols and rifles at Woburn, Massachusetts.

Tillman, J. N. about 1860. General gunsmith at Petersburg, Indiana.

Tisdale, Luther W. 1845–1865. Made percussion target rifles at Scranton, Pennsylvania.

Todd, George H. 1857–1865. General gunsmith at Montgomery, Alabama. Later had Confederate States contract for percussion rifles and brass frame revolvers patterned after Colt models.

Toledo Firearms Co. 1871–1880. Plant located at Toledo, Ohio. Made metallic cartridge revolvers of small caliber.

Tomes & Co., Henry 1847–1870. Gunsmith and dealer at 6 Maiden Lane, New York, New York. Made percussion shotguns and imported cased shotguns and revolvers from England. Became Tomes & Melvain & Co., in 1865.

Tonks, Joseph 1854–1867. General gunsmith at Boston, Massachusetts. Shop located at 37 Union Street, 1854 to 1857, and at 49 Union Street, 1857 to 1867.

Tooker, J. S. about 1850. General gunsmith at Carthage, New York.

Toulson, Alexander about 1670. Established a gunsmithery at St. Marys, Maryland Colony.

Town, Benjamin about 1775. Shop located at Philadelphia, Pennsylvania. Made flintlock muskets for the Pennsylvania Militia.

Towsey, Thomas 1791–1802. Shop located at Vergennes, Vermont. Had United States Government contract for Model 1795 flintlock muskets.

Trant, George B. 1873–1880. General gunsmith at Thornville, Ohio.

Trenton Arms Co. 1858–1868. Plant located at Trenton, New Jersey. Had United States Government contract for Model 1861 percussion rifles.

Tripper, A. N. about 1850. Made percussion hunting rifles at Potsdam, New York.

Trout, John 1855–1875. General gunsmith at Williamsport, Pennsylvania. Made percussion hunting rifles.

Troyer, William about 1845. Shop located at Lancaster, Pennsylvania. General gunsmith.

Truby, Jacob 1859–1861. General gunsmith in Drake County, Ohio.

True & Davis about 1860. Made percussion shotguns at Albany, New York.

Truitt Bros. about 1850. Shop located in Philadelphia, Pennsylvania. Made heavy caliber percussion rifles.

Trump, J. V. about 1840. Made cased percussion dueling pistols at Philadelphia, Pennsylvania.

Trumpler, J. F. about 1855. General gunsmith and dealer at Little Rock, Arkansas.

Tryon, George W. 1811–1878. George W. Tryon, born 1791 in Philadelphia, Pennsylvania, was apprenticed to the gunshop of Getz in Philadelphia and, in 1811, became a partner. The partnership was called Tryon & Getz, shop located at 165 North Second Street, 1811 to 1830, and George W. Tryon & Co., 134 North Second Street, 1830 to 1864. At this time he took his brother, Edward K. Tryon, into the business, and the name became Tryon Bros. & Co., 1864 to 1868. George W. Tryon, Jr., was also in the business at this time. George W. Tryon, Sr., died in 1878 and George W. Tryon, Jr., died in 1888. Edward K. Tryon, Sr., died in 1892. Edward K. Tryon, Jr., was also in the business. He died in 1905. From 1868 to 1905 the firm was known as Edward K. Tryon Co. This span of years covered from the flintlock through the percussion and into the metallic cartridge period of firearms. The earliest arms of Tryon were flintlock Kentucky rifles of fine workmanship and design; later, about 1835, they had a United States Government contract for trade muskets for the Indian Department. During the Civil War, the company had a number of United States Government contracts for percussion rifles and pistols.

Tubbs, J. B. about 1855. Made percussion rifles and shotguns at Waterloo, New York.

Tucker, Sherrod & Co. 1862–1864. Labon E. Tucker and J. H. Sherrod established a shop at Lancaster, Dallas County, Texas. They had a contract with the State of Texas for the manufacture of percussion revolvers, these to be patterned after the Colt models for the Army .44 caliber and the Navy .36 caliber. Their arms did not pass the Ordnance Board for the State, and the contract was canceled. The company continued to manufacture arms for civilian sale, and these were used by Texas officers in the Civil War. Some of these revolvers had a silver star set in either side of the wood grip.

Tunx, William 1769–1775. Established a gunsmithery at New York, New York. Returned to London, England, in 1775.

Turk, James 1852–1865. General gunsmith at Morrow, Ohio.

Turnbull, W. J. about 1885. Made metallic cartridge revolvers at New Orleans, Louisiana.

Turner & Ross 1873–1885. Shop and dealer at 16 Dock Square, Boston, Massachusetts. Sold metallic cartridge revolvers made under Turner and Ross name and to their specifications by the Whitney Company at Whitneyville, Connecticut.

Tyler Armory 1862–1865. Operated by Short, Biscoe & Co. at Tyler, Smith County, Texas. Awarded a contract on November 5, 1862, by the Military Board of the State of Texas, for percussion rifles. This contract was later taken over by the Confederate States Government.

Tyler, John 1772–1780. General gunsmith on Arch Street, Philadelphia, Pennsylvania, 1772 to 1775. Then moved to Allentown, Pennsylvania, 1775 to 1780.

Tyler, N. B. 1855–1871. Known as the Tyler Rifle Works at Vienna, Ohio. Made percussion Kentucky rifles, also heavy caliber percussion "Plains" rifles.

Tyler, William 1788–1802. Had United States Government contract for Model 1795 flintlock muskets at Providence, Rhode Island.

NOTES

Uhlinger & Co., W. L. about 1880. Made small caliber pocket metallic cartridge revolvers at Philadelphia, Pennsylvania.

Ullrich, Andrew 1855–1861. Made percussion rifles and shotguns at 197 Broad Street, Albany, New York.

Unger, Oswald 1858–1867. General gunsmith on Butler Street, Port Huron, Michigan.

Union Arms Co. 1858–1865. Plant located at 2 Central Row, Hartford, Connecticut, and office in New York, New York. Made percussion pepperboxes and had United States Government contract for percussion rifles and revolvers.

Union Rifle Works 1850–1860. Plant located at North Second Street, Philadelphia, Pennsylvania. Made percussion rifles.

United States Arms Co. 1870–1878. Plant located at 244 Plymouth Street, Brooklyn, New York. Made single-shot metallic cartridge pistols and small caliber revolvers.

Unverzagt, William 1868–1875. General gunsmith at Memphis, Tennessee.

Utter, George N. about 1850. Made saw-handle percussion pistols at Newark, New Jersey.

NOTES

Vagen & Co., J. H. 1869–1874. Made percussion rifles at Indianapolis, Indiana.

Valle, P. 1826–1840. General gunsmith at Second and Walnut Streets, Philadelphia, Pennsylvania.

Vandenburgh, O. B. 1858–1866. Shop located at Findlay, Ohio. General gunsmith.

Vanderburgh, William & E. 1848–1861. General gunsmith at Wilmington, Ohio.

Vandergrift, Isaac & Jeremiah 1809–1814. Shop located at Philadelphia, Pennsylvania. General gunsmith.

Vanderheyden, John about 1850. General gunsmith at Auburn, New York.

Vanderpoel, about 1740. Established a gunsmithery at Albany, New York Colony.

Vanderwaters, Hendrich about 1755. General gunsmith at New York, New York.

Van Horn, S. A. 1850–1880. Made heavy caliber percussion rifles of fine workmanship at Madison Street, Oneida, New York.

Vantrees, J. & J. F. (Son) 1826–1855. Percussion Kentucky rifle makers at Fort Recovery, Ohio.

Van Valkenburgh, S. about 1850. General gunsmith at Albany, New York.

Varner, John about 1800. Shop located at St. Clair Township, Allegheny County, Pennsylvania. General gunsmith.

Varney, David M. 1842–1875. General gunsmith at Burlington, Vermont.

Vaughn, I. S. about 1860. Shop at Main Street, Le Roy, New York. General gunsmith.

Vaughn, James M. about 1840. Shop located at Rutland, Vermont. General gunsmith.

Vickers, Jonathan about 1820. General gunsmith at Cleveland, Ohio.

Viergutz, Otto H. 1874–1880. Shop located at Pueblo, Colorado. General gunsmith.

Villwock, Charles 1860–1882. General gunsmith at Toledo, Ohio, 1860 to 1874. Under the name of **Villwock & Orth**, 1874 to 1882.

Vincent, Andrew 1857–1862. Shop located at Defiance, Ohio. General gunsmith.

Vincent, John & John Caleb (Son) 1844–1898. General gunsmiths at Vincent, Washington County, Ohio. John, Sr., active 1844 to 1882; John Caleb active 1882 to 1898.

Virginia Armory 1801–1865. In 1801, the State of Virginia authorized a manufactory and arsenal at Richmond, Virginia, to make arms for the Virginia Militia. Until 1820, flintlock muskets, rifles, and pistols were made there. From 1820 to 1860 it was used as a depot. In 1861, equipment and machinery from the Harpers Ferry Arsenal were shipped there and the manufacture of percussion rifles and pistols started under the Confederate States Government. The production continued until 1865. These rifles were marked "Richmond C.S."

Vocelle, A. about 1850. General gunsmith at 50 State Street, Charleston, South Carolina.

Voester, F. G. 1868–1875. Shop located at Denver, Colorado. General gunsmith.

Vogeler, Christopher & John (Nephew) 1784-1808. Flintlock Kentucky rifle makers at Salem, North Carolina.

Vogelsang, Henry about 1845. General gunsmith at 242 Washington, Street, St. Louis, Missouri.

Voigt, Henry about 1775. Maker of flintlock muskets for the Pennsylvania Militia at Philadelphia, Pennsylvania.

Volcanic Repeating Arms Co. 1854-1857. Organized June 20, 1854, with plant at Norwich, Connecticut. Principal stockholder was Oliver F. Winchester. Plant moved to New Haven, Connecticut, in February 1856. Name changed to **New Haven Arms Co.** April 25, 1857, at New Haven until 1866, when they moved to Bridgeport, Connecticut. **Winchester Repeating Arms Co.** took over the New Haven Arms Co. in 1867, and moved back to New Haven, Connecticut, in March 1871. Made "Volcanic" pistol.

Volvert about 1775. Made flintlock Kentucky rifles for the Pennsylvania Rifle Regiments at Lancaster, Pennsylvania.

Vondergrift, John about 1775. Shop located in Bucks County, Pennsylvania. Made flintlock muskets for the Pennsylvania Militia.

Vondersmith 1775-1783. Flintlock Kentucky rifle maker at Lancaster, Pennsylvania.

Vossburg, S. about 1845. General gunsmith at Albany, New York.

NOTES

Waechler, Louis about 1845. General gunsmith at 144 Franklin Street, St. Louis, Missouri.

Wakeman, Harvey 1828–1835. Shop located at Buffalo, New York. General gunsmith.

Walch Firearms Co. 1859–1864. Owned by J. Walch. Plant located in Brooklyn, New York and office at Park Row, New York, New York. Under date of February 8, 1859, patented a 10-shot and 12-shot percussion revolver, in which the cylinders took two loads per chamber. A few of these were made under United States Government contract, the 10-shot revolver as an Army model and the 12-shot as a Navy model.

Waldren, Alexander & William (Brothers) about 1670. Established a general gunsmithery at Boston, Massachusetts Bay Colony.

Walker, John about 1805. General gunsmith at Lancaster, Pennsylvania.

Walker, S. L. 1854–1889. Shop located at Cedarville, Ohio. General gunsmith.

Wallace & Osborne about 1850. Makers of percussion pistols at Canton, Connecticut.

Wallace, Victor M. about 1835. General gunsmith at West Topham, Vermont.

Wallach, Moses A. 1800–1825. General gunsmith at Boston, Massachusetts.

Wallis & Birch about 1850. Made percussion derringer-type pistols at Philadelphia, Pennsylvania.

Wallis, Daniel 1862–1864. Shop located at Talladega, Alabama. Had Confederate States contract for percussion rifles.

Walsh, James & John (Brothers) 1760–1779. Shop located in Philadelphia and Allentown, Pennsylvania. Made flintlock muskets and pistols for the Pennsylvania Militia.

Walsh, James 1861–1864. Shop and dealer at 60 Main Street, Richmond, Virginia. Smuggled Colt percussion revolvers to the Confederate States. His name stamped on some arms.

Walters, A. about 1825. General gunsmith at New York, New York.

Want, Edward 1861–1864. Shop located at New Berne, North Carolina. Had Confederate States contract for percussion pistols.

Ward, H. about 1850. Made percussion hunting rifles at Jamestown, North Carolina.

Ware, Joseph & Orlando (Brothers) about 1850. General gunsmiths at 145 Main Street, Worcester, Massachusetts.

Warner, Charles about 1860. General gunsmith at Windsor Locks, Connecticut.

Warner, Horace 1860–1890. Maker of percussion hunting rifles at Syracuse, New York, 1860 to 1879. Partnership of **Warner & Lowe** (William V. Lowe) at same location, 1879 to 1881. Horace Warner moved to Ridgeway (near Williamsport), Pennsylvania, in 1881, active until 1890. Made percussion target and match rifles of fine workmanship.

Warner, James 1851–1866. Shop located at Lyman and Gardener Streets, Springfield, Massachusetts. Made percussion and, later, metallic cartridge revolvers and carbines under his patent, dated January 7, 1851. Had United States Government contracts during the Civil War.

Warner, Joseph about 1830. General gunsmith at Philadelphia, Pennsylvania.

Warren & Steele about 1840. Made saw-handle percussion pistols at Albany, New York.

Washington Arms Co. 1849–1860. Made percussion pistols and pepperboxes at New York, New York.

Wassman, F. about 1850. Made percussion target and match rifles at Washington, District of Columbia.

Waters, 1775–1779. Shop located in Dutchess County, New York. Made flintlock muskets for the New York Militia.

Waters, Asa & Andrus (Brothers) 1775–1814. Established a gunsmithery and forge on Blackstone Creek at Sutton, near Millbury, Massachusetts. Made flintlock muskets for the Massachusetts Militia. Andrus Waters died in 1778. On September 8, 1808, Asa Waters, Sr., received a United States Government contract for 5000 flintlock muskets, and these were delivered by October 7, 1812. They were marked with a spread eagle over "U.S." and the word "Sutton" between the cock and the pan, and the year delivered to the rear of the cock. Asa Waters died December 24, 1814. The gunshop was carried on by Asa Waters' two sons, Asa, Jr., and Elijah, who had been apprenticed to the shop. Elijah died in 1814, the same year as his father. On August 31, 1816, Asa, Jr., received a United States Government contract for 5000 flintlock muskets. These were marked "U.S." over "A. Waters" between the cock and the pan, and, in the rear of the cock, "Millbury" and the year delivered. In 1818, Asa, Jr., also received a United States patent for the welding of gun barrels. On October 16, 1818, and January 2, 1825, he received United States Government contracts, each for 10,000 flintlock muskets. On September 22, 1836, he received a government contract for 4000 Model 1836 flintlock dragoon pistols. These were marked on the lock plate the same as the muskets, except "Milbury" was spelled with one *l*. Asa Waters, Jr., took his son, Asa H. Waters, into the business in 1840, and the name became **A. Waters & Son.** Under this name a United States Government contract was awarded on February 7, 1840, for 10,000 Model 1836 (changed from flintlock to percussion) pistols. Asa Waters, Jr., died in 1841. In 1844, the name was changed to **A. H. Waters & Co.,** and arms were so marked after this date, with "Milbury Mass." The company closed in 1855.

Waters, Richard about 1635. Established a gunsmithery at Salem, Massachusetts Bay Colony.

Watkeys, Henry 1772–1776. Shop located at New Windsor, Orange County, New York. Made flintlock muskets for the Continental troops.

Watson, Jonathan about 1800. General gunsmith at Chester, New Hampshire.

Watt, John about 1850. Maker of percussion Kentucky and match rifles at Mifflentown, Juniata County, Pennsylvania.

Watters, John 1778–1785. General gunsmith at Carlisle, Pennsylvania.

Weaver, H. B. about 1855. General gunsmith at Windham, Connecticut.

Weaver, Hugh about 1870. Shop located at Pleasant Ridge, Ohio. General gunsmith.

Weaver, Zachariah about 1845. Shop located at 11 Main Street, Rochester, New York.

Weeks, D. about 1850. Maker of percussion hunting rifles at Erie, Pennsylvania.

Weidman, Solomon about 1855. Percussion Kentucky rifle maker at Lancaster, Pennsylvania.

Weisgerber, A. about 1855. General gunsmith and dealer at Memphis, Tennessee. Made derringer-type percussion pistols.

Weiss, William 1802–1821. Flintlock Kentucky rifle maker at Lancaster, Pennsylvania.

Welch, Brown & Co. 1861–1865. William W. Welch and P. Brown had United States Government contract for Model 1861 percussion rifle at Norwalk, Connecticut.

Weller, Jesse 1858–1861. General gunsmith in Noble County, Ohio.

Welsh, James about 1780. Maker of flintlock pistols at Philadelphia, Pennsylvania.

Welshantz, Conrad, David, Jacob & Joseph (Brothers) 1777–1811. Shop located at York, Pennsylvania. Made flintlock muskets for the Pennsylvania Militia, also flintlock Kentucky rifles for individual trade.

Welton, Ard 1788–1801. General gunsmith at Waterbury, Connecticut. Had United States Government contract for Model 1795 flintlock muskets.

Welzdofer, Joseph about 1845. General gunsmith at 307 Main Street, Buffalo, New York.

Werner, J. G. about 1850. Made percussion hunting rifles at York, Pennsylvania.

Werner, Charles 1861–1875. General gunsmith at 43 Front Street, Rochester, New York.

Wesle, N. about 1855. General gunsmith at Milwaukee, Wisconsin.

Wesson, Daniel Baird 1843–1906. Born in 1829 at Worcester, Massachusetts. Entered the gunshop of his brother, Edwin, in 1843 at Northboro, Massachusetts, and at his brother's death in 1850, succeeded him in the business. In 1854, he formed a partnership with Horace Smith, establishing **Smith & Wesson** at Springfield, Massachusetts. D. B. Wesson died at Springfield, Massachusetts, August 4, 1906.

Wesson, Edwin 1838–1850. Shop located at Northboro, Massachusetts. Made Daniel Leavitt patent (April 29, 1837) percussion revolvers.

Wesson, Frank 1850–1877. Made percussion and, later, metallic cartridge pistols, carbines and rifles under the N. S. Harrington patents (October 25, 1859) and his own patents (November 11, 1862) at 15 Center Street, Worcester, Massachusetts, 1850 to 1870. Moved to Springfield, Massachusetts, 1870 to 1877. Had United States Government contract for metallic cartridge carbines. (Brother of D. B. and Edwin Wesson.)

West, B. B. about 1845. General gunsmith at Talcott Street, Hartford, Connecticut.

West, Stephen about 1775. Shop located in Frederick County, Maryland. Made flintlock muskets for the Maryland Militia.

Western Arms Co. about 1865. Made percussion and metallic cartridge revolvers of small caliber at New York, New York.

Westphall, Charles 1806–1814. Had United States Government contract for Model 1808 flintlock muskets at Philadelphia, Pennsylvania.

Weyerman, Isaac 1860–1868. General gunsmith in Le Sueur, Minnesota.

Whail, William 1813–1819. Shop located at Boston, Massachusetts. General gunsmith.

Wheeler, A. G. & G. E. (Son) 1865–1877. General gunsmiths and percussion hunting rifle makers at Farmington, Maine. A. G. active 1865 to 1868. G. E. active 1868 to 1877.

Wheeler, George 1787–1802. Shop located at Stevensburg, Culpepper County, Virginia. Had Virginia State contract for flintlock muskets for Virginia Militia.

Whetcroft, William about 1775. Maker of flintlock muskets for the Maryland Militia at Annapolis, Maryland.

Whipple, T. S. about 1855. General gunsmith at Cambridge, Vermont.

Whiston, Ephrem about 1820. Shop located at 119 Mulberry Street, New York, New York. General gunsmith.

White, George about 1800. General gunsmith at New Brunswick, New Jersey.

White, Horace about 1775. Made flintlock muskets for the Massachusetts Militia at Springfield, Massachusetts.

White, H. W. & J. A. 1851–1865. Made percussion Kentucky rifles of fine workmanship at Jackson, Ohio.

White, John about 1850. General gunsmith at 46 St. Clair Street, Pittsburgh, Pennsylvania.

White, Nicholas about 1800. Had United States Government contract for Model 1795 flintlock muskets. Shop located at Frederick Town, Maryland.

White, Rollin 1854–1868. Born June 6, 1817, at Williamstown, Vermont. Established the **Rollin White Arms** Co. at Lowell, Massachusetts, in 1854. Patented (April 3, 1855) a revolver with cylinder bored end-to-end with a special cartridge. Firm name changed to **Lowell Arms Co.** in 1866 and bought by **Smith & Wesson** in 1868.

Whitescarver, Campbell & Co. 1861–1864. Had Texas State contract for Model 1841 percussion rifles for Texas troops in Confederate Army. Plant located at Rusk, Cherokee County, Texas.

Whitemore, Nathaniel 1851–1872. Shop located at Marshfield, Plymouth County, and 4 Washington Street, Boston, Massachusetts. Made percussion rifles of fine workmanship and presentation pieces.

Whitmore, Andrew E. 1868–1877. General gunsmith at Somerville, Massachusetts.

Whitmore, N. J. about 1855. Made heavy caliber percussion match rifles at Potsdam, New York.

Whitmore & Wolf about 1850. Made percussion Kentucky rifles and pistols at Pittsburgh, Pennsylvania.

Whitney, Eli 1798–1825. Born December 8, 1765, at Westboro, Worcester County, Massachusetts. Invented the cotton gin on March 4, 1794. In 1797, he started to build and design machinery for a gunshop on the Mill River about two miles north of New Haven, Connecticut, and called the development Whitneyville, Connecticut. His first United States Government contract was June 14, 1798, for an adaption of the Charleville (French) flintlock musket. This arm was 57½ inches over-all; barrel, 42¾ inches; weight with bayonet, 9 pounds. Marked on lock plate with spread eagle over "New Haven" between the cock and pan. To the rear of the cock in a curve across the plate "U. States."

This contract was completed in 1809. The musket is known as the Whitney Model 1798. The second government contract was dated July 18, 1812, for a flintlock musket, over-all length 56½ inches; barrel, 41¾ inches; and weight, 9 pounds. Besides the United States proofmarks on the barrel, these were marked on lock plate between cock and pan in a scroll "N. Haven." The latter part of 1812, Eli Whitney took his two nephews, P. and E. W. Blake, into the business. On August 15, 1822, he entered into his third contract with the government. These were for a flintlock musket known as the Model of 1822. On January 8, 1825, Eli Whitney died at New Haven and was buried there. P. and E. W. Blake carried on the business and the latter part of the Model 1822 contract flintlock muskets were marked on the lock plate between the cock and the pan "U.S." over "P. & E. W. Blake" and "New Haven," with the year of delivery behind the cock. Eli Whitney, Jr., came into control of the business in 1841 and in 1842 received a government contract for the Whitney Navy percussion musket, which was the first percussion made by Whitney. The next government contract was for the Model 1841 percussion rifle, often referred to as the "Mississippi" or "Yager" rifle. In 1847, Samuel Colt supervised the manufacture of the Colt Army Model 1847 percussion revolver at the Whitneyville Armory. The **Whitney Arms Co.** continued to receive government contracts, and the muskets, rifles, revolvers, and carbines made at Whitneyville Armory covered the period from the flintlock musket to the magazine metallic cartridge rifle. The last rifles made were Kennedy magazine rifles, patented January 7, 1873. The plant closed in 1888.

Whitney, John about 1865. General gunsmith at Independence, Iowa.

Whittemore, Amos 1775–1785. Shop located at Boston, Massachusetts. Made flintlock muskets for the Massachusetts Militia.

Whittemore, D. about 1860. General gunsmith at Cambridge, Massachusetts.

Whittier, Otis W. about 1840. Made percussion rifles at Enfield, New Hampshire.

Whyley, Luther about 1845. General gunsmith at Portland, Maine.

Wickham, M. T. 1811–1836. Had United States Government contract for Model 1821 flintlock muskets. Shop located at Third and Noble Streets, Philadelphia, Pennsylvania.

Wickham, Thomas about 1775. Maker of flintlock muskets at Philadelphia, Pennsylvania, for the Pennsylvania and New Jersey Militia.

Wigfal, Samuel 1770–1776. Shop located at Philadelphia, Pennsylvania. Made flintlock muskets for the Pennsylvania Militia.

Wigit, Dominick 1857–1890. General gunsmith at Highland, Illinois, 1857 to 1884. Moved to St. Louis, Missouri, 1884 to 1890.

Wigle, Peter 1775–1780. Shop located in York County, Pennsylvania. Made flintlock muskets for the Pennsylvania Militia.

Wilcocks, John 1775–1780. Made flintlock muskets for the North Carolina Militia. Shop located at Deep River, North Carolina.

Wild, L. about 1840. General gunsmith at Brattleboro, Vermont.

Wilder, R. M. about 1865. Percussion rifle maker at Coldwater, Michigan.

Wilhelm, Jacob about 1855. Percussion Kentucky rifle maker at Lancaster, Pennsylvania.

Wilkins, Joseph about 1765. General gunsmith on King Street, Charleston, South Carolina.

Wilkinson, J. D. about 1865. Shop located at Plattsburg, New York. Made percussion hunting rifles.

Wilks, John about 1815. General gunsmith on Capitol Street, Albany, New York.

Willard, A. about 1860. Made percussion rifles at Boston, Massachusetts.

Willard, Bartholomew, about 1850. General gunsmith at Burlington, Vermont.

Willerding, about 1865. Maker of percussion pistols at Evansville, Indiana.

Willess, William about 1770. General gunsmith at Church Street, Norfolk, Virginia.

Willets, A. & S. about 1800. Shop located at New York, New York. Made flintlock rifles and fowling pieces.

Williams, Abraham about 1845. General gunsmith at Covington, Kentucky.

Williams, Elie about 1800. Made Model 1795 flintlock muskets under United States Government contract at Williamsport, Maryland.

Williamson, Argyle 1790–1807. General gunsmith at Charleston, South Carolina.

Williamson, David 1866–1873. Invented and patented (October 2, 1866) a breech-loading metallic cartridge derringer-type pistol at New York, New York. These were made by the National Arms Company of Brooklyn, New York, which he controlled.

Willis, John about 1775. Made flintlock muskets for Pennsylvania Militia at Philadelphia, Pennsylvania.

Willis, Richard about 1775. General gunsmith in York County, Pennsylvania.

Willis, William about 1770. Shop located at Williamsburg, Virginia. General gunsmith.

Wilmot, Nathaniel N. 1852–1867. General gunsmith at Boston, Massachusetts, 1852 to 1862. Then migrated to St. Paul, Minnesota, and established a shop at 362 Third Street, 1862 to 1867.

Wilson & Evans 1856–1865. H. H. Wilson and John R. Evans, general gunsmiths, dealers, and importers at 513 Clay Street, San Francisco, California.

Wilson, Samuel 1835–1855. General gunsmith in Fairchild County, Connecticut.

Wilson, T. about 1870. Shop located at Philadelphia, Pennsylvania. Made heavy caliber percussion rifles.

Wilt, J. 1850–1854. General gunsmith at Dayton, Ohio.

Winchester Repeating Arms Co. 1867 to date. Founded at New Haven, Connecticut, by Oliver F. Winchester, who had acquired control of the **Volcanic Repeating Arms Co.** and the B. Tyler Henry patent of October 16, 1860, which was the basic patent of the now famous Winchester rifle.

Winger, Richard 1774–1778. Made flintlock muskets in Lancaster County, Pennsylvania, for the Pennsylvania Militia.

Wingert, William & John (Brothers) 1845–1867. Shop located at 10 Congress Street, Detroit, Michigan. Made percussion pistols and rifles.

Winner, James 1805–1815. Shop located at 104 Walnut Street, Philadelphia, Pennsylvania. Also under the name of **Winner, Nippes & Co.** with shop at Mill Creek, Philadelphia, Pennsylvania, had United States Government contract for Model 1808 flintlock muskets.

Wintafeld, Abraham about 1815. General gunsmith at 427 North Third Street, Philadelphia, Pennsylvania.

Winter, Gustave about 1875. Shop located at Denver, Colorado. General gunsmith.

Winters, Elisha about 1775. Shop located at Chester Town, Maryland. Made flintlock muskets for the Maryland Militia.

Winters, John about 1845. General gunsmith at Walnut Street, Cincinnati, Ohio.

Winterstein, E. 1873–1880. Shop located at Trinidad, Colorado. General gunsmith.

Withers, Michael 1775–1805. Shop located in Lancaster County, Pennsylvania. Made flintlock muskets for the Pennsylvania Militia.

Witman, Solomon about 1855. General gunsmith at Lancaster, Pennsylvania.

Wolf, Adam about 1805. General gunsmith at North Square, Boston, Massachusetts.

Wolf, L. P. 1849–1854. Shop located at Ithaca, Ohio. General gunsmith.

Wolfe, Meredith 1853–1880. General gunsmith at Georgia Street, Chattanooga, Tennessee.

Wolfheimer, Philip about 1780. Flintlock Kentucky rifle maker at Lancaster, Pennsylvania.

Wood, Amos P. about 1855. Maker of percussion target pistols at New York, New York.

Wood, B. C. about 1860. General gunsmith at Syracuse, New York. Made percussion rifles and pistols.

Wood, J. B. about 1865. Shop located at Norwich, New York. General gunsmith.

Wood, John & John, Jr. 1724–1805. General gunsmithery at Boston, Massachusetts Colony 1724 to 1770. Succeeded by John, Jr., who moved to Roxbury, Massachusetts, 1770 to 1800, when he moved back to Boston. Active until 1805.

Wood, Josiah about 1775. Shop located at Norrington, Pennsylvania. Made flintlock muskets for the Pennsylvania Militia.

Woodbury, Crayton A. 1864–1868. Made percussion hunting rifles at Woodstock, Vermont.

Woods, James about 1800. Flintlock Kentucky rifle maker at Lancaster, Pennsylvania.

Woods, John 1768–1775. Emigrated from England, set up a gunsmithery at New York, New York. Returned to England in 1775.

Woods, Luke about 1810. Shop located at Sutton, Massachusetts. Had United States Government contract for Model 1808 flintlock muskets.

Woods, Thomas about 1810. General gunsmith at Philadelphia, Pennsylvania.

Woodward, Gilman 1849–1860. Made percussion hunting rifles at Keene, New Hampshire.

Workman, J. about 1850. General gunsmith at Hamburg, Pennsylvania.

Worley, Henry 1859–1870. General gunsmith in Berks County, Pennsylvania.

Wright, A. 1853–1865. Shop located at Newburgh, New York. Made percussion hunting rifles.

Wright, Alba C. about 1850. General gunsmith at Fitchburg, Massachusetts.

Wright, Alexander 1835–1846. General gunsmith at Poughkeepsie, New York.

Wright Arms Co. about 1870. Made small caliber metallic cartridge revolvers at Lawrence, Massachusetts.

Wright, Henry A. about 1835. General gunsmith on Main Street, Buffalo, New York.

Wrisley, Loren H. 1834–1851. Made flintlock and later percussion hunting rifles at Norway, Maine.

Wuerke, F. 1869–1875. General gunsmith at Alton, Illinois.

Wurfflein, Andrew & William (Son) 1835–1900. The father, Andrew Wurfflein, established a gunshop at 335 North Third Street, Philadelphia, Pennsylvania, in 1835 and was located there until 1850, when he moved to 122 North Second Street, 1850 to 1860, and then to 208 North Second Street, 1860 to 1871. His son, William, took over the business in 1871 at this address and continued until 1900. The Wurffleins were dealers and custom gunmakers of all types of firearms through the percussion and metallic cartridge periods. They were famous for their fine workmanship on percussion sporting and target rifles. Also, percussion presentation derringer-type pistols and cased dueling pistols.

Wylie, William about 1805. General gunsmith at 73 Church Street, Charleston, South Carolina.

NOTES

Yager, Charles about 1865. General gunsmith at Lancaster, Pennsylvania.

Yahner, H. F. about 1850. Maker of percussion Kentucky rifles in Cambria County, Pennsylvania.

Yard, Benjamin about 1775. Made flintlock muskets for the New Jersey Militia at Trenton, New Jersey.

Yearin, Adam about 1805. General gunsmith at Scotio, Ohio.

Yeisley, Henry 1857–1866. Shop located at Lucas, Ohio. Made percussion hunting rifles.

Yerian, L. M. about 1885. General gunsmith at Cumberland, Ohio.

Yost, Caspar 1773–1778. Made flintlock muskets and rifles for the Pennsylvania regiments. Shop in Lancaster County, Pennsylvania.

Yost, John 1775–1783. Shop located at Georgetown, Maryland. Made flintlock muskets for the Maryland Militia.

Youmans, about 1775. Flintlock Kentucky rifle maker at Lancaster, Pennsylvania.

Young, D. about 1850. General gunsmith at Middleburg, Pennsylvania.

Young & Co., H. about 1860. Made percussion pistols at New York, New York.

Young, Henry & John (Brothers) 1774–1783. Shop located at Easton, Pennsylvania. Made flintlock rifles and pistols under contract for the Continental Congress and, later, the United States Government; also custom work. Fine workmanship on flintlock holster pistols.

Young, John 1728–1740. Armorer to Maryland Colony. Location of shop not recorded.

Young, Peter about 1800. General gunsmith at 37 North Second Street, Philadelphia, Pennsylvania.

Young & Smith about 1850. Made percussion pepperboxes in New York, New York.

NOTES

Zahm, Matthias about 1815. Flintlock Kentucky rifle maker at Lancaster, Pennsylvania.

Zartman, Joshua 1852–1888. General gunsmith at 77 North Fifth Street, Newark, Ohio.

Zeeck, Andrew 1850–1880. Shop located at New Madison, Ohio. General gunsmith.

Zettler, C. J. & B. (Brothers) 1868–1890. Shop located at 134 Bowery, New York, New York, 1868 to 1874, then moved to 107 Ewen Street, Brooklyn, New York, 1874 to 1890. Made metallic cartridge target rifles and pistols of fine accuracy and workmanship.

Zettler, John about 1850. General gunsmith at 71 Allen Street, New York, New York.

Ziegler, H. D. 1858–1866. Shop located at Portsmouth, Ohio. General gunsmith.

Zimmerman, F. C. 1872–1890. Emigrated to the United States from Germany in 1863. Worked as a gunsmith as he migrated West. Set up his own shop at Dodge City, Kansas, 1872 to 1890.

Zittle, Frederick about 1835. General gunsmith on Elm Street, Buffalo, New York.

Zollinger, George about 1840. Percussion Kentucky rifle maker at Carlisle, Pennsylvania.

Zorger, Frederick & George (Brothers) 1770–1802. Made flintlock pistols and Kentucky rifles at York, Pennsylvania.

Zuendorff, John 1850–1864. General gunsmith at 106 East Houston Street, New York, New York.

NOTES

Gilbert Forbes,

Gun Maker.

At the Sign of the Sportsman in the Broad Way,
opposite Hull's tavern in New-York.

MAKES and sells all sorts of guns, in the neatest
and best manner, on the lowest terms; has
also for sale, silver and brass mounted pistols, rifle
barrel guns, double swivel and double roller gun
locks, common do. 50 ready made new bayonet
guns, all of one size and pattern.

NOTES

A. Important first patent dates are shown. Improvement patent dates are not shown unless they were a radical departure from the original patent.

B. Regarding the span of years a gunmaker was active, I have been conservative on the known data, and there may be a possibility of "before and after" in the years shown.

C. Letters, initials, or code marks on some firearms: It is difficult to determine whether these are makers', owners', or inspectors' marks; and such data can sometimes be determined by their location on the piece. If a letter or group of letters are stamped on the face of the lock plate, these may be the maker's code; but in most cases the maker was proud of his workmanship and used his name. The owner's initials or name often appeared on a silver or brass plate on the butt. This is true particularly of pistols. If the piece was made under Federal or State Government contract, the inspector's initial or code letter was usually stamped on the barrel with the "P" or proofmark. Some inspectors also stamped their initials on the side of the butt stock, after the piece had been completely proved and inspected. Regimental numeral and company letter were sometimes stamped on the tang of the butt plate. If a gunmaker bought his barrels from an outside source, the barrelmaker often stamped his initial or code mark on the underside of the barrel. This, of course, is not visible until the barrel is removed from the stock. This may also be the case where locks were made for the gunmaker, and a code mark may be found on the inside of the lock plate.

D. Now that still mooted question, shall we call it a "Pennsylvania Rifle" or a "Kentucky Rifle"? There is no question the former is quite correct; but, nevertheless, through the years "Kentucky Rifle" has developed as a generic term describing the long flintlock or percussion rifle and is more commonly used to designate a piece of this type. It is true the Pennsylvania gunsmiths made this type of rifle years before the frontiersmen opened up the Kentucky territory. I have used both terms to satisfy both schools of thought.

APPENDIX

CHRONOLOGY OF AMERICAN FIREARMS

1630: Eltweed Pomeroy established a gunsmithery at Dorchester, Massachusetts Bay Colony.

1635: Bennett and Packson earliest known gunsmiths in Maryland Colony. Gunsmithery on Kent Island.

1646: Covert Barent established a gunsmithery at New Amsterdam (New York).

1685: John Hawkins established a gunsmithery at Charles Town, Carolina Colony.

1697: Theophilus Munson established a gunsmithery at New Haven, Connecticut Colony.

1710: Martin Meylin, earliest known flintlock Pennsylvania rifle maker in the Lancaster, Pennsylvania, area.

1728: Earliest known dated flintlock Kentucky rifle by J. Metzger, Lancaster, Pennsylvania Colony.

1742: Stephen Evans established a gunsmithery at Mt. Joy (near Valley Forge), Pennsylvania Colony.

1750: John Cookson made a multi-shot flintlock musket of 9 charges, one charge behind the other, at Boston, Massachusetts Colony.

September 9, 1776: Congress declared that the name "United Colonies" be changed to "United States." All lock plates shortly after this date on government-made or government-contracted firearms were marked "U.S." or "U. States."

1795: Springfield (Massachusetts) Armory produced its first arms.

June 14, 1798: Eli Whitney received his first United States Government contract for flintlock muskets at Whitneyville, Connecticut.

March 9, 1799: Simeon North received his first United States Government contract for 500 flintlock dragoon pistols at Berlin, Connecticut.

1801: Harpers Ferry (West Virginia) Armory produced its first arms.

1810: Elisha Hayden Collier developed a flintlock revolving-cylinder pistol at Boston, Massachusetts.

1811: Captain John H. Hall patented a successful flintlock breech-loading arm.

1812: First government proofmarks were used, "P" for proved and "U.S."

1816: Joshua Shaw of Philadelphia, Pennsylvania, developed the copper percussion cap.

1831: Henry Deringer developed his short rifled barrel, large caliber percussion pistol at Philadelphia, Pennsylvania.

1834: Ethan Allen patented the pepperbox type of pistol.

February 25, 1836: Samuel Colt awarded a United States patent for his percussion revolver.

March 5, 1836: Charter granted Patent Arms Manufacturing Company at Paterson, New Jersey.

1855: First percussion Springfield rifle adapted to use the Minie bullet invented by Colonel Rossi Minie of the French Army.

July 22, 1856: C. S. Pettingill received a United States patent for his double-action hammerless percussion revolver.

October 16, 1860: B. Tyler Henry received a United States patent for the lever-action metallic cartridge rifle, later the Winchester.

April 20, 1897: John M. Browning of Ogden, Utah, patented the action that the Colt Company use in their automatic pistol.

BIBLIOGRAPHY

American Art Association Sales Catalogues.
American Arms and Arms Makers, by Robert E. Gardner.
American Gun Makers, by L. D. Satterlee and Major Arcadi Gluckman.
Early American Gunsmiths, by Henry J. Kauffman.
Anderson Galleries Sales Catalogues.
Breechloader in the Service, by Claude E. Fuller.
History of Browning Guns from 1831. Browning Arms Company.
Francis Bannerman Sons Catalogues.
Henry Deringer's Pocket Pistol, by John E. Parsons.
Encyclopedia of American Hand Arms, by George Morgan Chinn and Bayless
    Evans Hardin.
Firearms in American History, by Charles Winthrop Sawyer.
Firearms of the Confederacy, by Claude E. Fuller and Richard D. Steuart.
The First Frontier, by R. V. Coleman.
The Gun and Its Development, by W. W. Greener.
History of Firearms, by Major H. P. C. Pollard.
Hand Cannon to Automatic, by Herschel C. Logan.
History of the United States Army, by William Addleman Ganoe.
The Kentucky Rifle, by Captain John G. W. Dillin.
Muzzle-loading Rifle, by Walter M. Cline.
Notes on United States Ordnance—Small Arms, by Major James E. Hicks.
Simeon North, by S. N. D. North.
The Nunnemacher Collection, vols. I & II, by John Metschl.
Our Rifles, by Charles Winthrop Sawyer.
Percussion Colt Revolver and Conversions, by John E. Parsons.
Parke-Bernet Galleries Sales Catalogues.
The Peacemaker and Its Rivals, by John E. Parsons.
Pepperbox Firearms, by Lewis Winant.
Pistols, Their History and Development, by James Frith.
Royal United Service Museum Catalogue (London).
Remarks on Rifle Guns, by Ezekiel Baker.
The Revolver, by Patrick Edward Dove.

Remington Handguns, by Charles Lee Karr.

Smith & Wesson Handguns, by Roy C. McHenry and Walter F. Roper.

Sharps Rifle, by Winston O. Smith.

Nathan Starr, by Major James E. Hicks.

Sotheby Sales Catalogues (London).

United States Martial Pistols and Revolvers, by Major Arcadi Gluckman.

United States Muskets, Rifles and Carbines, by Major Arcadi Gluckman.

Weapons and Equipment of Early U. S. Soldiers. United States Department of Interior.

Whitney Firearms, by Claude E. Fuller.

Wallis & Wallis Sales Catalogues (Lewes, England).

Walpole Galleries Sales Catalogues.

Yankee Arms Maker, by Jack Rohan.

Journal of the Company of Military Collectors and Historians.

Various old town and city directories.

ILLUSTRATIVE PLATES

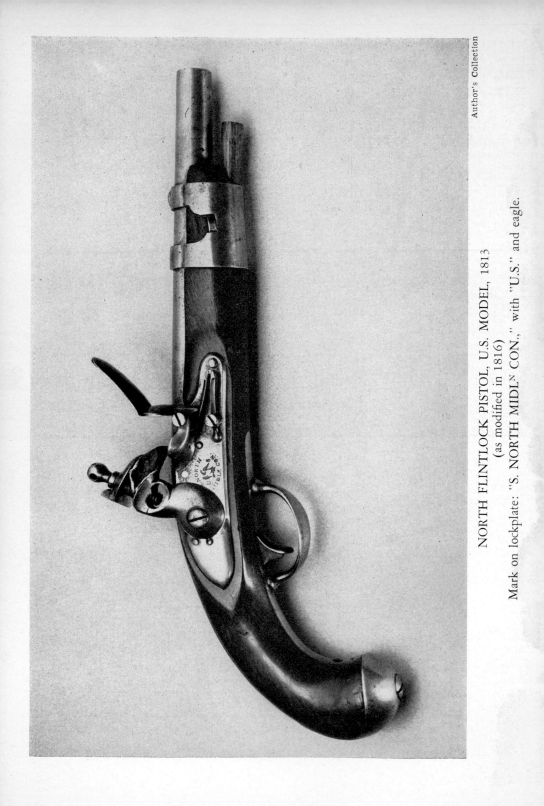

NORTH FLINTLOCK PISTOL, U.S. MODEL, 1813
(as modified in 1816)

Mark on lockplate: "S. NORTH MIDL^N CON.," with "U.S." and eagle.

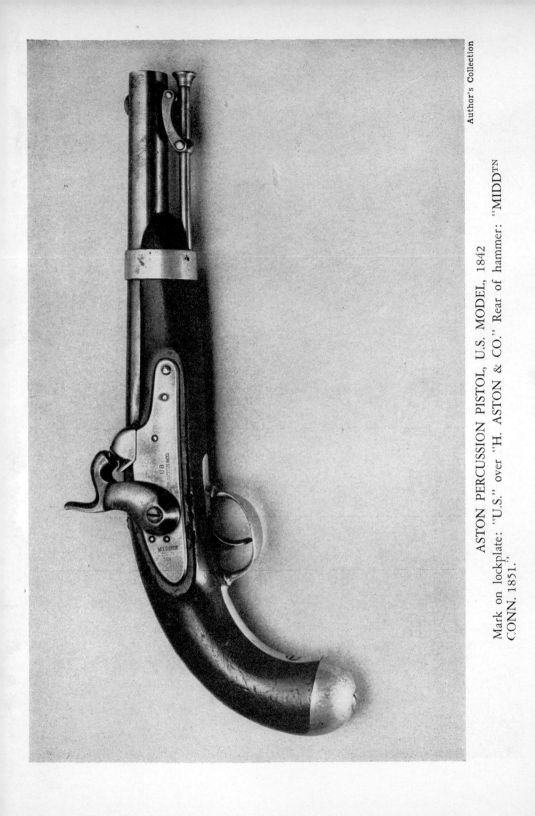

ASTON PERCUSSION PISTOL, U.S. MODEL, 1842

Mark on lockplate: "U.S." over "H. ASTON & CO." Rear of hammer: "MIDD^{TN}
CONN. 1851."

COLT DRAGOON—SECOND U.S. MODEL OF 1848

Mark on barrel: "ADDRESS SAMᴸ COLT NEW YORK CITY." On frame: "COLT'S PATENT" over "U.S." On cylinder: "MODEL U.S.M.R. [United States Mounted Rifles] COLT'S PATENT." Made about 1851.

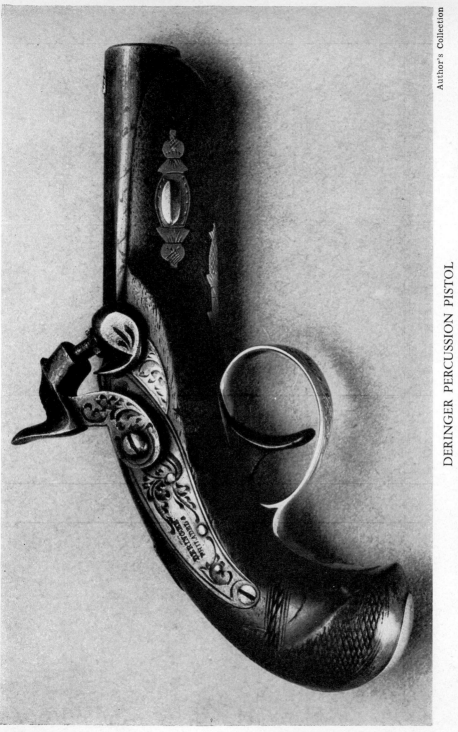

DERINGER PERCUSSION PISTOL

Mark on lockplate: "DERINGER PHILADELA." On barrel: "DERINGER PHILA-
DELA." and "N. CURRY & BRᵒ. SAN FRANCᵒ CALᴬ AGENTS." Made about 1864.

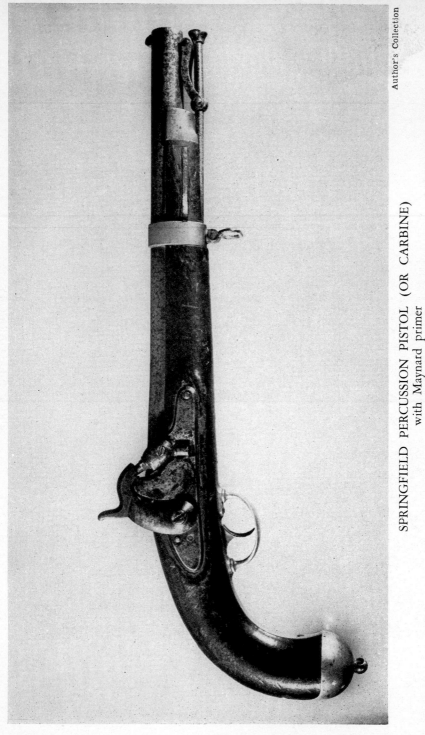

SPRINGFIELD PERCUSSION PISTOL (OR CARBINE)
with Maynard primer

Mark on lockplate: "U.S." over "SPRINGFIELD," spread eagle with shield and "1856."
Stamped "8" on tang of butt plate. Slots for shoulder stock attachment.

SPRINGFIELD ARMORY
Springfield, Massachusetts, 1860.

Courtesy Americana Foundation

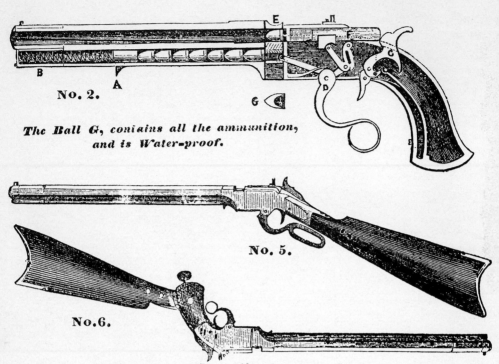

NO. 2.

The Ball G, contains all the ammunition, and is Water-proof.

NO. 5.

No. 6.

No. 2 or 6 inch barrel Pistol, 7 balls, 66 to the pound.—*See Sectional View.*
No. 3 or 8 inch barrel Pistol, 9 balls, 66 to the pound.
No. 5 or 16½ inch barrel Rifle Carbine, 20 balls, 66 to the pound.
No. 6 or 16½ inch barrel Detached Breech Rifle Carbine, 20 balls, 66 to the pound.

DIRECTIONS.—*See No. 2.*

Push the spring up in the tube by the knob A, till the top or cap B can be turned to the left, then put the cartridges (ten or less) in the tube, replace the cap B, when the spring will follow the cartridge down, raise the hammer C, and swing the lever D CLEAR forward, which will elevate the carrier E with a cartridge, pull the lever D clear back, which forces the cartridge into the barrel and braces the breech-pin F, when the arm is in condition for discharge.   In case of mis-fire bring up another ball.

Circulars with prices at wholesale and retail, can be had by addressing J. W. POST, 229 *Broadway, N. Y.*, Sole Agent for the sale of the Volcanic Repeating Fire-Arms for the U. States.

COLT'S
PATENT REPEATING PISTOLS,
Army, Navy and Pocket Sizes,
RIFLES AND CARBINES,
MANUFACTURED AT
HARTFORD, CONN.
☞ Beware of Counterfeits and Patent Infringements. ☜